THE 401K OWNERS MANUAL

George A. Huss

ISBN-10: 0996478809
ISBN-13: 978-0-9964788-0-9

I am honored to dedicate this book to my daughter.
She is so much more than I was at her age.
I cannot wait to see what her future will hold.

Acknowledgments

Thanks to everyone who has walked with me on this journey. If I have done anything remotely unique, I believe I have taken the influence of many talented experts from unrelated fields and blended their wisdom to craft a relevant solution for you. There are so many wonderful people who have inspired me. I especially want to mention several people by name.

Frank I. Luntz, whom I have followed on social media for some time, deserves my particular gratitude. I am indebted to him for opening my eyes about how today's young people feel about their future. His work was the inspiration for the opening of this book. I hope some day we will get to shake hands. You can get to know more about him at www.luntzglobal.com.

Daniel Gilbert is Professor of Psychology at Harvard University. Another giant in his own field. His book titled "Stumbling on Happiness" was particularly relevant and inspiring. Can you find happiness? You really can. Check him out at http://www.wjh.harvard.edu/~dtg/gilbert.htm

Lin and Larry Pardey are giants in the world of blue water sailing. I have been following their travels for years now. Their relevance to this book is demonstrating a life anyone can emulate. Their books and their generous sharing of their experience continues to be a personal inspiration. Lin, in particular, has inspired my own writing. Hopefully, Lin will publish a few more books on their adventures. Thanks Lin. Check them out at http://www.landlpardey.com/

Edward "Ted" Siedle is the master of pension forensics, on the constant lookout for conflicts of interest, excessive and hidden fees and champion of the retirement plan participant. I thought I knew most everything there was to know about how Wall Street worked. Ted showed me more. You can find him and his extensive work at http://www.benchmarkalert.com/

Brené Brown is an Author and a professor at The University of Houston. Her research on vulnerability, courage, shame, and authenticity all helped me recognize the human elements of what is actually going on with plan participants. I am an ardent fan of her work and have drawn so much strength from her wisdom. Thank you, Brené. Perhaps some day we can sit and talk. I would encourage you to look her up at http://brenebrown.com/

Greg Mankiw is Chairman and Professor of Economics at Harvard University. His research on the growth rate of time actually spent in retirement is relevant to us all.

Lauren R. Rublin has my many thanks for a piece she wrote in April 13th, 1998 about over-diversification of investment portfolios. She is now Deputy Managing Editor at Barron's.

Rolf Dobelli is a novelist, thinker and author of The Art of Thinking Clearly. I love his work to help us all understand that news, all news, is a product. It makes us passive and destroys creativity. You can find his work at http://www.dobelli.com/

Barry Ritholtz is not your typical Wall Street persona. He's an author, newspaper columnist, equities analyst, Chief Investment Officer of Ritholtz Wealth Management, and guest commentator on Bloomberg Television. It is refreshing when an expert in the field tells the truth even if the financial media doesn't want to hear it. If you want more, you can find him at http://www.ritholtz.com/blog/

Seth Godin, described as an author, entrepreneur, marketer, and public speaker. To me he is one of those rare individuals who not only understands human nature, he is not afraid to speak the truth. I am indebted to him for describing so eloquently how we talk, negatively, to ourselves about issues which are important to us. You won't regret spending time with him on his blog at http://www.sethgodin.com/sg/

Not a person, per se, but thanks to StockCharts.com for permission to use a few of their charts as an introduction to Point & Figure Charting.

And, finally, I must express my personal gratitude to Tom Dorsey. The investment methodology I'll share with you at the end of the book, Point & Figure Charting, has been used by Wall Street insiders now for over 130 years. Tom personally introduced it to me. His passion for the methodology is legend and he inspired me to find every book ever written on the topic.

Tom Dorsey co-founded Dorsey, Wright & Associates in 1987. He is the author of Point & Figure Charting: The Essential Application for Forecasting and Tracking Market Prices, Thriving as a Broker in the 21st Century and Tom Dorsey's Trading Tips: A Playbook for Stock Market Success.

Tom has become a giant in the area of Point & Figure Charting because of his firm's contributions to the advancement of the method as it is used today. In particular is the application of Relative Strength Analysis in the management of investment portfolios.

Most all I know about Point & Figure Charting I've learned from Tom, his books and my daily use of Dorsey, Wright & Associates research for over twenty-two years. For decades now, I've studied not only Tom's work but the writings of earlier practitioners and have updated charts every day, by hand. I wouldn't consider using anything else.

If you want to find out more about Tom, check out DorseyWright.com

Contents

Chapter One - Start at the End
Introduction
Start at the End 1
The Power of Imagination 2
How to Add Reality to Imaginings 3
Kickstarting the Process 6
Storm Tactics 8

Chapter Two - Savings
Introduction
Pay Yourself First 12
Saving without Sacrifice 14

Chapter Three - Understanding your 401k Options
Introduction
401k Investment Options 17
Bond Funds 20
Target Date Funds 23
Target Date Funds - Continued 27
The Future of Target Date Funds 29
The Secret Formula that (nearly) Destroyed Your 401k 30
How to cure Asset Allocation Anguish 33
Steal this 401k Tip 36
Company Stock 38
The Self-Directed Brokerage Option 38

Chapter Four - The Plan Provider & Your Company
Introduction
The Secrets of the 401(k) Industry 41
The Letter of the Law 44
But You Are Not Helpless 46
Plan Providers Play to the Status Quo 47
Hidden Transfer of Risk to the Plan Participant 51
What's "Fair" for Plan Participants 52

Company Communications 54
What They Tell You (or Don't) is Important 55
The Risk Tolerance Question 57
How You are Viewed by Plan Providers 58

Chapter Five - Understanding Your Role
Introduction TO DO
How You Ended Up With 401k a Plan 61
Are You Getting Advice 65
Common Obstacles You can Overcome 68
Pandering to Safety 70
Why Your Role is Critical 73
Focus on What's Important 74
The #1 Investor Challenge of Today 78
The Seven Deadly Investment Mind-Games 80
Master or Slave 83
What Do People Really Want 84
Discovering Choices 86

Chapter Six - Forensic Discoveries
Introduction
There will Never be "More" Time 88
Beware the Law of Averages 90
Expectations 92
Whose Market are You Watching 95
Everyone Gets Fired 97
Headline Risk 99
Unintended Consequences 101
The Overdose Risk 103
You cannot "Opt-Out" of Risk 105
Not Your Childhood Piggy-Bank 106
The Common Sense Principal of Investing 109
The News is Bad 110
The Fee Frenzy 113
When Fees Are a Big Deal 116
Blind Faith 119

Write it Down 121
The Buddhist Key to Investing 123
Trash Talk 126
Beliefs Have Consequences 128
Managing the Downside 130
Inevitable Boom and Bust 131
The Map and the Territory 133
There is a Solution 135

Chapter Seven - Measure What's Important

Introduction
Point & Figure Charting 137
American Funds Growth Fund of America 140
Euro Pacific Growth Fund 146
Davis New York Venture Fund 151
Fidelity Contrafund 154
Vanguard 500 Index Fund 159
NYSE Bullish Percent Index 163
Bullish Percent Concept 166
Positive Trend Analysis 170
Relative Strength Analysis 170

Chapter Eight - Final Thoughts

Final Thoughts 175

DOWNLOAD MP3 OF THE FIRST CHAPTER FREE!

READ THIS FIRST

The First Chapter contains the key idea on how to focus your thinking about retirement. Having it handy as an audio file will make it simple to use as often as you wish.

So, just to say thanks, I'd like to give you the downloadable MP3 of the First Chapter 100% FREE!

CLICK HERE TO DOWNLOAD

(Or, just go to www.GeorgeHuss.com for the download.)

Chapter One
Start at the End

The ability to imagine is the greatest power of the human brain. It does not require money or credentials. Imagination knows no limits. It is yours for the taking; but, take it you must or life will be a cruel master.

xoxoxo

Start at the End

We all know, in a really general way, it's a good idea to think about retirement.

Yet, thinking about retirement in a really *general* way (or not at all) is, in my opinion, the single greatest obstacle to having a successful retirement outcome because...

1. A *general* idea (or none at all) about your own retirement makes it too easy to put off participating in your plan.

2. A *general* idea (or none at all) about your own retirement makes it too easy to convince yourself it's ok to cash out your retirement plan if you change employers.

3. A *general* idea (or none at all) about your own retirement makes it too easy to think it's ok to borrow money from your retirement plan.

4. A *general* idea (or none at all) about your own retirement makes it too easy to tell yourself you will never retire.

Each of these symptoms of having a *general* idea (or none at all) about your own retirement will increase the risk that you will run out of money during your normal retirement years. I can think of nothing more frightening.

That's the reason I want to start this journey with you... at the end.

You deserve security and stability when it comes to your retirement. This peace of mind comes from knowing what you want.

The first step is to imagine what it will be like for you in retirement. What you believe will have consequences. So it is important to help you paint a detailed picture of you as the main character in your retirement story. Do not dismiss this idea because you think it is unlikely. Remember, beliefs have consequences. If you believe retirement is unlikely for you, it will become a self fulfilling wish.

All you need to do is answer three easy questions.

Where are you? Who are you with? What are you doing?

The great thing about this is there is no limit to what you imagine. The only "rule" is it must be specific. This is a fun exercise you can do for free! Revisit it as often as you like. In fact, you should revisit it often. You can change the picture as many times as you like. It is your story. It is personal and relevant and unique to you alone.

By answering these simple questions, you can begin to frame a future designed to bring you nothing less than happiness. Spend as much time as you like imagining.
And, I'll help you do it better.

First of all, relax because this is not another lecture about creating and sticking to a budget. What I am suggesting is to take your powerful imagination and picture, in as much detail as you can, exactly how your retirement will look. The point is to create a future so appealing to you, personally, that a shift in your thinking may take place.

The shift I'm talking about is a change in attitude from struggle and sacrifice to joyful anticipation. Perhaps this is not what you were expecting from this book. If not, skip this section altogether or come back to it later. Or, you may want to read a little further.

xoxoxo

The Power of Imagination

The human brain is nothing short of remarkable. The mind, the subconscious mind, is incapable of distinguishing between a real and an imagined event. So taking the time to imagine your retirement triggers your brain to make changes and reinforces whatever steps necessary to actually make it real.

One way you can do this is to write a letter to yourself written from the perspective of your future self. In it you will be describing the future you are experiencing.

Remember the three questions: Where are you? Who are you with? What are you doing? Describe the answers in as much detail as you can. Describe where you are living. Describe your dream home. Describe the climate. Describe the colors. Describe the aroma. Describe the people. Describe what you and everyone around you are doing. Get the idea?

The more detail you can add the greater the shift in your thinking. Remember, the idea is to make this so very appealing that your attitudes around the actions to get you there will change.

I saw a very impressive advertisement once which posed the question: "Suppose there was someone who would gladly pay you to do exactly what you love?" The answer was: there is. That person is you. All you are doing during your working career is getting the money together to pay yourself… to do exactly what you love for the rest of your life.

If you write the letter I mentioned on a computer or a mobile device, you can, and should, revisit it. Perhaps it would be a fun Saturday morning exercise. Or, perhaps you could play with it waiting for an appointment or while waiting in a long checkout line.

One online tool you may find useful is called Evernote. You can get an individual Evernote account free of charge. It's a cloud based digital workspace you can use to collect ideas about your retirement. A "note" can be most anything. It can be formatted text, a webpage, a photograph, a voice memo, or a note you create. You can then use these notes as research to help create the voice of future you.

If you see a picture of a house you love, copy and paste it to Evernote. If you see an article describing a place where you would like to live in retirement, copy and paste it to Evernote. Or, you may just copy the link to the article. Get the idea? The more detail you use in your story the more effective it will be to get you there.

xoxoxo

How to Add Reality to Imaginings

While we are all capable of imagining, there is one very important activity you can use to boost your retirement outcome. It is based on the scientific research from a Harvard Professor. His name is Daniel Gilbert. He detailed his research in a book titled "Stumbling on Happiness."

The summary of his findings are as follows: When we imagine future circumstances, we fill in details that won't really come to pass, and leave out details that will.

In the second half of the book Gilbert identifies what he calls a psychological immune system. A healthy psychological immune system strikes a balance that allows us to feel good enough to cope with our situation; but, we feel bad enough to do something about it.

The way I would describe this is: we make up stories. Stories where we manufacture our own happiness. Let me explain. Ever lose something? A job, a special relationship, or a thing you were attached to? Do you notice that now, as you look back on it, it wasn't so bad; or, you now say you are grateful for what the experience taught you?

Can you see this is a story you made up, after the fact? Had you written your thoughts about the experience while it was happening and compare those past thoughts with your present feelings you would see they don't match.

This is how we cope. Grieving for a loss is fine; but, reliving that loss day after day only serves to make day to day living difficult, and in the extreme, impossible for some. So a healthy psychological immune system helps us make up stories about the past.

As for the future, the psychological immune system is quick to manufacture positive and credible views of how the future will unfold; however, the science shows we make up stories in detail about things that won't really come to pass, leaving out details that will.

For example, have you ever bought an investment which lost money? Did you continue to hold the investment and tell yourself "It'll come back. I'll just wait until the market realizes I'm right."

When you think about it, that really makes sense because we are manufacturing a story about something we have not experienced and so what we do is take building blocks from the past and the present and assume they will continue into the future.

Now, this is where the science may be of particular benefit to the 401(k) investor.

Participants reported in Gilbert's work that they believe they would have greater regret over an *action* resulting in a poor outcome. They stated they believe this regret would be greater than taking no action even if the poor outcome was the same.

Note, in this situation participants are imagining the future. However, and this is the kicker... *In the future, remembering this past event...* it was the inaction which they reported as being the greater regret.

Remember the way the psychological immune system works: the brain *can* manufacture positive and credible views of what we learned from an experience; but, it cannot when the result was from inaction because there was no experience.

So, the brain cannot make up a credible view, other than regret, because you took no action. Brilliant. You get to experience a negative outcome and you get to beat yourself up over it.

Gilbert suggests there is a solution to this dilemma and here it is... Seek out people who are currently experiencing a future you would like to experience and ask them to relay what it's like now.

Who is the oldest living person you know in retirement? First, write down their age because you may live longer; and, second, think about calling or visiting them. Ask them their story. What did they imagine their future would look like and ask them what it's like now. Ask them about what they would do differently. The answers may surprise you.

What Gilbert's science suggests to me, is we tend to hedge our bets when we should blunder forward. Future you will have less regret taking action than doing nothing.

If you are reluctant to seek out these people, remember, they are just like you, only older. And, I have found people, in general, are more than willing to talk about themselves. We love to tell our stories! And, I believe, people are generally willing to help. The benefit for you is they may point out details you never considered or may identify where your thinking may be distorted.

There is one other finding Gilbert offered which you should take to heart. We *mistakenly* believe that because something is hard to imagine it is *unlikely* to happen. In turn, we overpay for the opportunity to indulge our current outlook because we believe our current opinions will never change.

This is why I believe it is so important to imagine your future as positive and as wonderful as you can, even if your current thinking is it is unlikely. Our brains have a unique structure that allows us to mentally transport ourselves into future circumstances and allows us to feel what it is like to be there.

Again the solution to this dilemma is to seek out people who are currently experiencing a future you would like to experience. Ask them their story. What did they imagine their future would look like and ask them what it's like now. Ask them what they did to get there and what they would do differently.

xoxoxo

Kickstarting the Process

If you are having trouble kickstarting the process of imagining a future, allow me to make some suggestions which may get you started. At the very least, you may find these ideas offensive. Good. Sometimes finding out what we want begins by discovering what we do *not* want.

What I've laid out for you is the framework for imagining your future retirement. Some other things you may want to use to help your imagination: Try to imagine there are no limitations as to where you may live in retirement. Suppose, just suppose, you can live in an exotic location. Heck, we're imagining here, so why not beautiful, historic, romantic, and adventure filled along with exotic?

Imagine locations that:
1. are cheaper than the United States,
2. have great weather,
3. are safe,
4. have the best infrastructure,
5. have the best health care, and
6. are the most foreign-resident-friendly

Think of places like Panama, the South of France, Kuala Lumpur, Belize, Thailand and Nicaragua.

If you want to look into this further, check out Live and Invest Overseas on FaceBook. The Publisher's name is Kathleen Peddicord.

Kathleen has covered the live and invest overseas beat for more than 25 years and is considered the world's foremost authority on overseas retirement. She has traveled to more than 50 countries, invested in real estate in 17, established businesses in 7, renovated historic properties in 6, and educated her children in 4.

Full Disclosure: I have no financial interest in Kathleen's business. I get nothing if you choose to buy her publication or attend any seminar she may run or in which she may participate. I only bring this to you so you can start the process of thinking specifically rather than generally about your retirement.

I'll give you one other area to explore before we move forward.

Lin and Larry Pardey.

Lin and Larry are a married couple famous internationally for their expertise in small boat sailing. They have sailed over 200,000 miles together, having circumnavigated the world both east to west and west to east aboard self-built, wooden, engine-free cutters under 30 feet in length. They are Authors of a dozen books, countless magazine articles, and co-creators of five cruising documentaries. Lin and Larry have shared their sailing experiences with tens of thousands around the globe prompting many to take up the sport and live the dream of the cruising lifestyle. Their motto has always been, Go simple, go small, go now!

Check their website: http://www.landlpardey.com/

The reason I want to bring this couple to your attention is they began very early to create a remarkable life for themselves. Sailing can be a very expensive undertaking; however, Lin and Larry had a different approach.

You see, Larry was just a regular guy with the idea of seeing the world. He spent several years in Canada working a regular job; and, on the side, began fixing up old boats, sailing them and then selling them. In 1964 he went in search of his dream boat on the California coast. He failed.

Undeterred, he set out to build his own. It took him three years working on it part time and in the end, he and Lin decided to go on their first extended adventure… without an engine!

At that point, they had put 4,200 hours into the construction of their boat and paid $7,765 (1965 −1968) for materials. Why no engine? As Larry explained in "Cruising in Seraffyn" the cost of an engine would have been $2,500 which was equal to twelve months living and cruising expenses during their first trip to Mexico. So the decision was, either give up a year of freedom or have an engine. Without one, they learned how to better plan and navigate and sail their craft.

The other point I want to share with you is Larry basically did what I'm suggesting you consider doing. He talked extensively with others who could help him with his dream. He took the time to share his ideas, was willing to learn along the way and was willing to expand his ideas based on the experience of others who had been there. You see, Lin and Larry did not invent this lifestyle. Many had come before them. They just took the best others had discovered on their own and made it part of their dream.

In the process, Lin and Larry made their own discoveries and were willing to share them with those who were to follow. Most notable in my mind is Larry's contribution in his Storm Tactics Handbook. In it he explains how to survive hurricane force wind and heavy seas using tactics many modern sailors overlooked… to their ultimate peril. Some of these tactics, in my opinion, are fantastic principals for every day life, including investing.

xoxoxo

Storm Tactics

1. If you are reluctant to make direct contact with someone who is currently living the future you imagine, one other choice may be to read what others have written. I read most all of Lin & Larry's works before I had the courage to send Lin an e-mail. I was delighted when she responded.

2. Larry is a great example of someone who has examined the experience of others, applied their experience, improved upon it and shared what he learned.

I've included my thoughts from The 401(k) Owners Manual, Podcast Episode 80, titled "Rode Trip," to highlight these two ideas.

Most of you don't know that I am an arm-chair sailor. I love sailing stories. For my 50th birthday, I gave myself the gift of sailing lessons and absolutely adored it. Unfortunately, I've not spent any time on-board since. However, I love reading about it. If you are ever looking for a good read, I have a suggestion for you. Lin and Larry Pardey.

Lin and Larry currently live in New Zealand. I had the chance to meet them both in Annapolis, Maryland, a short while ago, when they were promoting their latest book. It was perfect. A tiny book shop and perhaps twelve to fifteen invited guests got to hear Lin talk about their adventures.

The first four of their books are about their sailing adventures from the very beginning which I would recommend to anyone. I love the way they write and they do know how to tell a story. The fifth publication to their credit is a handbook on storm tactics.

And this is the topic for today. Storm Tactics: The thing my friends brought out in their handbook on surviving hurricane force storms in mid-ocean just makes so much sense.

Do everything in your power to stop the boat... so that the storm will pass. Obviously it's a bit more technical than that. But, this is the main idea of the handbook. In theory, even a simple squall moving at six knots and a boat trying to outrun the storm at six knots, in theory, would have you riding in the storm indefinitely. Alternatively, the way to spend the least amount of time in the storm is to stop and let it pass!

The handbook goes into great detail on the research of storms and the how-to's to keep boat and crew safe; and, isn't that what you want for yourself? How to keep safe during a stock market storm?

One of the tools you can use is a rode trip. That's r... o...d... e... Not r... o... a... d...

In sailing terms, in most cases, rope is a term used only for the raw material. Once a section of rope is designated for a particular purpose on a vessel, it generally gets it's own name. A rode is a special purpose line or rope, It's what attaches an anchored boat to its anchor. It may be made of chain, rope, or a combination of the two. An Anchor Trip-line has a two-fold purpose. The first is to warn other vessels in the harbor of the general location of your anchor so they do not accidentally cut your anchor loose or foul their propeller on your line. The second is to help retrieve your anchor if it should become stuck on the bottom.

One of the tips Lin and Larry offer in Storm Tactics is this: "If you are anywhere near land and there is any doubt you can reach a safe port before the blow sets in, alter course immediately to head offshore and gain searoom."

The Two key points here being "Safe" and "Searoom" because not every port is safe all the time. Case in point: In December of 1982 there were 45 cruising boats lying in the Cabo San Lucas anchorage. Cabo San Lucas is a city at the southern tip of the Baja California peninsula, in Mexico. It was a disaster waiting to happen, and happen it did. The weather broadcast mentioned a stalled cold front about 300 miles west of Cabo. Before it was over most all the boats ran a ground. Many a total loss. Few boats survived in what was considered to be a safe port. Those that did survive left port before the blow and rode out the storm in open waters where they had plenty of searoom.

Sound familiar? Didn't everyone believe they were safe in 2008? I remember clearly hearing major Wall Street firms saying stay the course. Ride it out. That didn't work for the world's best sailors in Cabo in 1982 and it didn't work for you either.

So consider using a rode trip. At least prepare yourself to raise your anchor and give yourself some searoom. Remember the same wisdom applies: Land is not a boat's friend. Boats are safest far from land. In kind, being invested at all times and in all markets is a sure way to run a ground. Like some of the vessels who tried to ride it out at Cabo in 1982, you may lose everything or suffer losses very difficult to repair.

Let me just say at this point, none of this is to suggest you take up Lin and Larry's lifestyle.

Just know that it is possible for you. People are still choosing this as part of their "retirement" dream. Lin mentioned in their October 2014 newsletter that she and Larry had just come ashore after sailing with two potential voyagers looking for advice on how to get started. "If we sell the house and my business, then find the right boat and buy it for X and can figure out how to live on Y per month, that's it, retired."

If this appeals to you, Lin and Larry have written extensively on the subject from detailed "how to" instructions to colorful and entertaining descriptions of their adventures under sail. Lin is a marvelous storyteller and I highly recommend everything the two of them have written.

Again, if you are reluctant to call or write to someone who is currently living the life you imagine in retirement, see if you can find those who have put their experience in writing.

The point here is to encourage you to seek out people who are currently experiencing a future you would like to experience. Learn everything you can. Use it to create a picture of your perfect life. This is the first and most important step on the journey to retirement.

Chapter Two
Savings

The future is unstoppable. It will come at you whether you prepare for it or not.

xoxoxo

Pay Yourself First

'Why do you want it?' 'How much will it cost?' 'Is it going to make your life better?'

If the first step for a retirement outcome is having a specific idea about what retirement is for you, then the next step is making a decision to save money in order to make that dream a reality.

If you remember only one thing from this section of the book, remember this…

Savings will have the single greatest impact on achieving a successful retirement.

1. It is more important than what investments are available in your plan.
2. It is more important than investment returns. And,
3. It is more important than whether or not your employer matches your contributions.

If there is any single idea that will benefit you… this is it. Pay yourself first.

OK, let's be clear. Paying yourself first does not mean taking money out of your income and putting it aside for a new plasma TV, luxury car, boat, watch, the latest and greatest cell phone or some other gadget, gismo or toy.

Paying yourself first means putting money aside for yourself so that you may have the freedom to choose not to work for money at some point in your life. The best way to save money is to contribute to your 401(k), especially if your company will match any of your contribution!

First, your contribution is not taxed when you put it in; and, second, if your employer matches any portion of your contribution, you just got a huge bonus. If you put in $1,000 over the year and your employer matches your contribution dollar for dollar you not only saved $1,000, you just made $1,000! I will do that all day long.

There are any number of excuses why you may not choose to do this. "Well, I do not plan to be with this company long. It is just the only thing I could get right now." "I would rather have the money in my pocket to spend the way I want." "I need all that money to live on."Face it… these are all just excuses.

The truth is it does not matter if you do not plan to be with the company a long time. If you leave your present employer, the 401(k) account may be transferable to your next employer or you can do a 401(k) rollover to an Individual Retirement Account or you can do a 401(k) rollover to Roth Individual Retirement Account. In the case of the 401(k) rollover to Roth, be sure you understand the tax issues before you do it.

If you are of the mindset that "I would rather have the money in my pocket to spend the way I want." You may want to be honest with yourself and ask if what you want is something you really need. Most likely it is not.

If you are in the camp that says "I need all that money to live on." Perhaps that is true – today. Here again, the answer may be taking an honest look at the way you spend money and determine what you really need. All too often I have found myself spending money needlessly.

Ask yourself these three simple questions before you spend your money…

'Why do I want it?' 'How much will it cost?' 'Is it going to make my life better?'

Taking the time to ask yourself these questions may create enough space for the desire to slip away.

This is so very important, it is worth repeating…

The *single* greatest factor which will lead to a successful retirement outcome is savings. Period.

Investment returns in an absolute sense are meaningless if you apply them to insignificant account balances. Think about it. Would you rather have a 20%

return on a $10,000 investment account or a 3% return on a $1,000,000 investment account. Remember, you cannot spend a percentage return.

So the first order of business is to save, especially if your company offers a matching contribution. If you are not saving enough to get the maximum matching contribution, it's no different than tossing your wallet into the street. You're throwing money away.

Think of it this way. What if there was someone who would pay you to do exactly what you love to do? Well, there is. That person is YOU. You will be the person who pays you to do what you love. You're just getting the money together to be able to do just that. The easiest way to save is to participate in your company's 401(k) plan because the money from your pay is removed before you ever see it.

xoxoxo

Saving without Sacrifice

So, let's talk about painless ways you can actually save money because this seems to be the number one reason people give for not participating in their 401(k) plan. The common answer is they "need" all their money today to meet living expenses.

In my opinion, saving for retirement can be done with joyful expectation. If you are looking at savings as a sacrifice or a struggle, resentments may build to the point that you simply give up. Never, never, never give up.

Obviously, a complete discussion of ways to save money are beyond the scope of this book. However, it is a popular topic on and off the internet and you should have no problem finding more tips than you can use. To get you started, I'll give you one tip and hopefully it will inspire you to go out and look for more ways you can improve the value of what you buy.

So here we go… Razor Blades.
If you shave on a regular basis, you probably spend a fair amount of money every month on replacement blades. Even if you use an electric razor, you may want to pay attention.

The industry has spent vast amounts of money developing blades. I recall the days when my father had a single blade razor. It was a butterfly safety razor. It had a twist to open mechanism on the bottom so insertion of a new blade was relatively safe and simple. As I recall, replacement blades were inexpensive and he replace them about once a week. Sometimes he replaced them sooner.

Safety razors today have been developed with thinner and thinner blades which are stacked with two, three, four and five blade shaving surfaces. The manufacturers claim that the thinner blades give you a better shave. Perhaps they do. However, let's think this through.

The major elements necessary to dull a metal blade and thus require replacement are water and oxygen. These two elements act to corrode the metal. This is what make's the blade dull. A dull blade will not move smoothly over the surface resulting in nicks and cuts.

The immediate user response is to replace the blade. The typical user shaves with water and then hangs the razor in the shower or by the sink. The thinner the cutting surface of the metal, the less surface there is to dull. The faster the blade dulls, the quicker the user replaces the blade. Coincidence? You decide.

So here's the tip: immediately after using the blade, submerse the blade in glycerine.

I have no doubt you have an old coffee mug in the kitchen. Go the to the store and buy a six ounce bottle of generic glycerin. You should be able to find it for under $4.00. Put just enough glycerin in the cup to cover the blades.

What you are doing, is depriving the blade surface of oxygen. Without oxygen the chemical reaction necessary to cause rust is stopped. It is rust which makes the blade dull.

I have been doing this for years now and I can tell you I typically use the same blade for no less than three months! I've extended the useful life even further by easily sharpening the blade. How? Once the blade begins to feel dull, I'll take the blade and sharpen it by placing a pair of denim jeans on the bed with the lower half of the pant legs facing up.

Then, I run the blade 20 or 30 times over the fabric surface in one direction and again in the opposite direction. This seems to work quite well because of the diamond shaped pattern in the denim weave.

This usually extends the life of the blade for at least another 30 days.

I can't tell you how much money this idea will save you because it depends on what kind of blades you use, where you normally buy them and how "tough" the hair is you are shaving. I would suggest, however, that this idea alone more than covered the amount you invested in this book!

The point here is not to lecture you. The point here is simply to help you think about ways you can painlessly make your income do more for you so you will not miss the money you pay yourself.

Google "money saving ideas at home" and you can pick and choose what you can do. I'm not suggesting you dive into Extreme Couponing or radically change your lifestyle. Just pick one or two ideas and try them. Perhaps the razor blade idea or cutting back on coffee shop purchases or making your own lunch once or more a week will work for you. If not, there are countless other ways, if you are willing to look. Future you will be grateful.

One final note, impulse purchases which appeal to your emotions rarely provide even short-term satisfaction of the desires they promised to achieve.

The goal of parts one and two of the 401(k) Owners Manual are simple. They are designed to provide you with some insights so that you can begin to take action.

Action is the key to change. From here, we will move to help you understand what investment options are available to you and how you can make better choices given the dynamic nature of investing in general. This is where the fun begins.

Chapter Three
Understanding your 401k Options

Awareness, you're half way there.

xoxoxo

The Big Picture

In this section, we are just going to look at what is inside your 401(k). Most plans have a number of investment choices on what is called the main menu. The latest surveys I've seen say there are about 18 mutual fund choices on average, 12 if you exclude Target date funds.

In addition to the main menu of investment choices, some plans may allow you to buy your company's stock, if you work for a publicly traded company.

Your plan may also have a self-directed option which will allow you to make investment choices other than the limited few offered on the main menu.

Ok, let's focus on the mutual fund choices on the main menu.

No doubt, someone in your human resources department gave you more information on these choices than you wanted. In addition to any description of the funds in your enrollment packet, you should have gotten a hard copy or online prospectus for each fund. A prospectus is a disclosure document required by securities law which most people don't understand; but, contains a great deal of valuable information.

There is no question this is an unbelievable amount of information for you to consume. At this point you likely feel this 401(k) of yours is more confusing than your company's health care benefits. You are not alone. I have heard the same opinion expressed by senior executives of Fortune 500 companies.

I believe this confusion was the catalyst for what may now be the default investment in your plan, The Target Date Retirement Fund, or life-cycle fund.

Prior to the creation of this product, plan participants had to choose from the mutual funds available, or their savings would wait in a money market account within the plan until they actually made a choice.

An industry survey conducted many years ago revealed that the money market account was where about a third of employees had "invested" their 401(k) savings. So, despite the best efforts of the plan provider and human resources to create effective education programs on how to properly invest 401(k) savings, it would seem employees were either unwilling or unable to make a choice.

This was not a good outcome. Not good for the employee, because money market returns over a working career won't be enough to fund retirement. Not good for your company, because they were not delivering a benefit to a large population of employees. And, it was not good for the plan provider, let's just say it was not good business. So, plan providers set out to change the rules, and succeeded.

Instead of you choosing where and when to invest your retirement savings account, many plans now state that unless you make a different choice, you will automatically be invested in a Target Date Retirement Fund, or life-cycle fund. I will do a separate discussion on Target Date Funds.

And, finally, that leaves the other mutual funds on the main menu.

These can be described as stock funds, bond funds and specialty type funds. Stock funds can be separated into a nine panel grid: Large-Cap value, Large-Cap blend, Large-Cap growth; Mid-Cap value, Mid-Cap blend, Mid-Cap growth; and, Small-Cap value, Small-Cap blend, Small-Cap growth. See a pattern?

Large, Mid and Small Cap simply identify the size of the public company the mutual fund managers are concentrating on. The theory being that large companies are lower risk because they are older, more established successful public companies. The Mid-Cap companies less so and the Small-Cap companies less so again.

The distinction between value, blend and growth, again, in theory, has to do with a measure of risk. A "value" company theoretically being less risky vs. a company on a fast growth track because the larger a company becomes the more difficult it is to maintain a fast growth rate.

The bond funds can also be separated into a nine panel grid with different measures: credit quality on one scale and interest rate sensitivity on the other.

For the 401(k) investor the important thing to know is that a bond fund is not the same as a bond because a bond fund lacks the one element which makes bonds generally regarded as a "safe" investment: that being a stated maturity date at which time the investor is at least promised the return of 100% of his or her investment.

No such promise exists in a bond fund despite the fact that something like 70% of all investors are unaware of the fact. This is really important, so I'll give it to you once more. You are never promised to get all of your investment back in a bond fund. Got it? Good.

Ok. The final mutual funds are specialty type funds and may include market index funds or real estate investment trusts. Again, it depends on what your company has approved for your plan.

The takeaway is Human Resources should be able to give you a document called "The Summary Plan Description" where you can see what your investment choices are. Hopefully you can find the same information in your enrollment packet.

I would suggest you list all the investment options in your plan; and, collect the ticker symbols for each choice. A ticker symbol is simply a unique way to represent a particular publicly traded security.

I will show you how you can use them to help rank the choices available in your plan. Mutual fund ticker symbols are generally a string of five letters. It is an easy way to collect information from places like the mutual fund company's Website, MSN, Lipper, Yahoo!, and of course, Morningstar.

If your company or your plan provider tells you there is no ticker symbol for one or more funds in your plan, it means that fund is not publicly traded. In which case you are at the mercy of the plan provider for any information on the fund and nothing I will share with you here will be of any help.

Unfortunately, there are still a few plan providers holding on to offering only house funds where they make the maximum profit. If there is not a self-directed option offered in your plan where you can use publicly traded investments, you are stuck with the fox guarding the henhouse.

xoxoxo

Bond Funds

In my opinion, it is critically important to lift the lid on the idea that bonds are a safe bet for your 401(k) retirement savings. One of the things I have seen in every 401(k) plan I've ever reviewed is a scale measuring investment risk from lowest to highest and the mutual fund choices available in the plan placed in the approximate location on that scale.

One example of the progression from low risk to high risk is represented as follows: cash; Bonds; Balanced; Large Company Stocks; Aggressive Stocks (Mid-and Small Cap); followed by International Stocks and other.

We need to focus on the "low risk" side of the scale. This will be important as we look at the other products offered in the plan. Cash is fairly self explanatory.

However the next on the risk scale is bonds and that is where we will focus our attention today. There is a subtle disconnect when the 401(k) investor looks at the risk scale and assumes the bonds as represented on the scale are the same as the bond funds offered in the plan.

This is a common misconception with bond funds in general. This asset class is typically represented as being low risk, the implication being that it is safe, although that is not always the case.

To understand this we need to look at one key risk of a bond investment. Interest rate risk: which is easy to understand. The rule is that Bond prices move inversely to interest rate changes. All that means is as interest rates go down, bond prices go up. And, in the reverse, as interest rates go up, bond prices go down.

For a bond owner interest rate risk is easily managed simply by holding the bond to maturity, when they are at least promised to get all their money back.

Let's take a simple example: Say Mary owns a bond which she bought when it was issued. She paid $100,000 for the bond; it had a 5 year maturity and a stated interest rate of 5%. So each year, Mary will get $5,000 of interest.

What happens at the end of the first year if interest rates go to 10%? Mary still gets $5,000 of interest; but, she sees that her friend Gail who just bought a $100,000 bond is getting $10,000 in interest income every year.

Mary likes the idea of $10,000 vs. $5,000. So she calls her broker and says I would like to sell my bond so I can get one with a better interest rate. Her broker crunches the numbers and says she can get Mary about $83,000 for her bond.

What?! Mary says. I paid $100,000 for that bond just last year!

So her broker explains that the current interest rate is now 10%. Anyone willing to buy a bond today can get 10%. So if she wants to sell, she will have to price her 5% bond so a buyer will yield about 10% in order to make it attractive vs. other bonds the buyer could easily get. The only way to do that is to lower the price so it will effectively yield 10%.

Now, Mary is depressed. She is thinking that her bond is only worth $83,000; however, her broker reminds her that at the end of 5 years, she is promised the return of the full $100,000; and, the reason she bought the bond was she wanted to be sure to have all that money in 5 years.

In a bond fund however, the investor never has a stated maturity date and there is no guarantee, or even promise, they will get all their money back.

The bonds inside the fund will mature and the corporation or government agency who is the bond issuer will very likely pay as promised; but, that is not how it plays out for the bond fund investor. So the bond fund investor cannot escape the interest rate risk and there is never a promise that they will get all their money back.

The planning question for the 401(k) investor has to be: are interest rates more likely to rise or fall from the time of my initial investment to the time I expect to cash in my retirement account?

If I am looking at a low interest rate environment when I put my money to work, and have ten or twenty years left until I retire, the question is how likely is it that interest rates will remain the same or go lower? Should they go higher, I may not get the return of my investment.

Are bond funds low on the risk scale? The answer depends on your view of interest rates.

Another risk bond and bond fund investors alike share is called inflation risk. Early in my career I heard bonds referred to as "certificates of confiscation" because the purchasing power of the future dollars returned to the bond owner is generally lower than when they put the money to work.

Inflation is simply a rise in the general level of prices of goods and services in an economy over a period of time. When the general price level rises, each dollar buys fewer goods and services. Today, most economists favor a low, steady rate of inflation (Low - as opposed to zero or negative inflation).

In the United States, the task of keeping the rate of inflation low and stable is given to The Federal Reserve. So for the 401(k) investor, the takeaway is that there will be inflation – and money invested in a bond fund over a working career will likely result in a loss of purchasing power.

If you are thinking this has nothing to do with you, you don't have to look back very far to see the effects of inflation:

In 1999: 7-11, Slurpee, largest... $0.99
Gallon of gasoline... $1.30
Aspirin, Bayer, 100-count... $3.47
5 lb. bag Sugar... $2.13(which today is only a 4lb bag)
1st class Stamp, USPS... $0.33

So, again, are bond funds low on the risk scale? The answer also depends on your view of inflation. Remember, it is not the job of the Federal Reserve to STOP inflation; it is to control the rate of growth of inflation. Inflation is real.

The last risk we will talk about for bond and bond fund investors is called Credit Risk. Simply put, it is a judgment around the issuers' ability to fulfill the promise to repay the bond at maturity and their ability to pay current and future interest on their debts.

For the 401(k) investor, this is important. The lower the credit rating, the higher the interest rate the issuer must offer to attract buyers of their bonds; but, the higher the risk the issuer will be unable to repay the investor.

Again, this is important not only for choosing bond funds offered in your plan but also, so called balanced funds that invest a portion of the portfolio in bonds; and, it is also important for the 401(k) investor who has their retirement savings in a Target Date Fund.

Again, because a portion of the Target Date Fund portfolio is invested in bonds.

Just to make this relevant to you. In 2010 I was reviewing a 401(k) plan with over 6,000 active participants and $167 million in plan assets as of year-end 2009; I noticed that roughly $44 million was in Target Date Funds.

There were eleven Target Date Funds in total, geared toward participants ranging from ages 25 to 75 years old. My analysis was not to check on the credit quality of the bond portfolio. I assumed they would all be AAA rated. This is supposed to be the "safe" portion of the Target Date Fund after all. To my surprise, what caught my immediate attention was, that not one of the eleven funds had a Triple A rated average credit quality!

More to the point, the seven funds geared toward participants ranging from ages 25 to 55 years old had an average credit quality below investment grade, what are commonly referred to as "Junk Bonds." The four funds geared toward participants ranging from ages 60 to 75 years old all had a BBB rating which, although the lowest possible rating to still qualify as "investment grade," the BBB rating is described by S&P as medium class borrowers, which are satisfactory - at the moment. I can't say anything other than AAA makes me feel all that "safe" thank you very much.

The takeaway for the 401(k) investor... are bond funds low on the risk scale? The answer also depends on the Credit Risk the fund manager has assumed.

Recall I encouraged you to collect the ticker symbols on all the investments available in your plan. With the ticker symbol you can go to Morningstar.com and easily look up the average credit quality of the bonds held in the fund portfolio and make your own judgment on how safely your money is being invested.

To wrap up: Interest rate risk, inflation risk and credit risk are real. So, don't be quick to make a snap judgment that bonds are a safe bet for your 401(k) retirement savings just because some graph in your 401(k) enrollment packet placed them low on the risk scale. It just isn't so.

xoxoxo

Target Date Funds

The first thing to be aware of is you may find yourself in a Target Date Fund without actually having made that investment choice yourself. Not too long ago, the rules were changed so that employers would be allowed to automatically invest your money in these products, unless you chose to opt-out, and make your own investment choices. And, I encourage you to do just that.

Something I've learned over the years is everyone has an agenda. I have an agenda, to help you make better 401(k) investment choices. You have an agenda, you want to know more about your 401(k). And, the simple truth is *if you don't have an agenda, someone else will have one for you.*

On topic, if you follow the money trail, think about how much more money is being charged by a mutual fund company inside Target Date Funds vs. Money Market Funds (the old default option). The fees are something like 10 times more in a Target Date Fund. Do you think there is an agenda to get you invested right away?

Listen, this product was designed as a one stop shop for employees to prevent them from getting "stuck" in the plan's money market account, which had been the 401(k) default investment, because historically, about one-third of employees were either unwilling or unable to choose from plan investments.

And, rather than spend time, talent and money to do a better job of educating employees, plans were offered a product as a solution. Why not create a profitable product vs. adding massive expense to better educate employees?

The "benefit" these mutual funds are selling is to rebalance the portfolio toward more conservative assets, over time, as the employee approaches retirement. Sounds like a good idea; but, what's really happening?

OK, before we go any further, let's look at the idea of "rebalancing." What a brilliant marketing word. You do know rebalancing is simply a word Wall Street adopted as marketing jargon?

Let me explain. I heard a story recently about someone who went to the Fence Company to get some batteries replaced. You know the company. The one that sells electric fences to keep your pet in the yard. Well, after the clerk replaced the batteries in the dog collar, the sales clerk mentioned to the customer: By the way, if you didn't know, the store is wired, so be careful how you hold the collars when you leave the store or you may get a "correction."

It took the customer a moment to understand, because what the clerk meant by "correction" was, you may get a severe electric shock!

You see, the Fence Company created a bit of marketing jargon in their business. Taking a common word, "correction" and using it to market and sell a benefit to potential customers.

They couldn't very well run an ad campaign telling people that for the safety of your pet, we've developed a system to administer a total body, brain numbing, electro-shock, behavior-modification treatment! No. it's just a "correction." That sounds so much more gentle and loving, doesn't it?

Get the idea? So, who doesn't want to be rebalanced?! Truly. If I find myself out of balance, I would love someone to help me get back to center. I have many friends I call on when I am troubled and need to get rebalanced and see things in their true perspective.

But what does your 401(k) plan mean when they use this term?

Well, rebalancing as used as a marketing term means, once a year on the anniversary of your employment or calendar year end or on whatever annual date the fund has identified (Why not Cinco de Mayo or Boxing Day?!) the fund automatically sells and buys something to create a predetermined mix of stock funds and bond funds in your account.

A quick sidebar: Remember, somebody on Wall Street makes money when there is buying and selling.

Forgive me. How does this automatic buying and selling make any sense in terms of the condition of the stock market or the bond market or the demonstrated direction of stock prices or interest rates on some arbitrary annual date? It doesn't.

The assumption being made here is that the stock portion of the portfolio will always be more risky then the bond portion of the portfolio. This is an assumption… that bond funds are the safety net. Yet, if history is any guide, and we have nothing else to go on, this is not always the case.

Remember the previous discussion about bond funds vs. bonds. A bond fund owner has no date when he or she is going to get back all of their money. The risk a bond fund owner cannot escape is the interest rate risk. If interest rates are rising, bond prices and bond funds are falling.

Let's go a little deeper.

Recall the Target Date Fund in your 401(k), in theory, is to protect your retirement savings account by rebalancing your portfolio every year, moving money out of the stock market and into bonds (bond funds, actually) increasing the percentage of bond funds in your account as you get closer to retirement age.

Let's assume, simply for the sake of discussion, that, based on your age and desired retirement date the Target Date Fund begins with a mix of 70% stocks and 30% bonds. On the first annual date for the Target Date Fund to rebalance, the new mix will be 65% stocks and 35% bonds.

On the date the Target Date Fund is to be rebalanced, does it matter if the stocks now represent 80% of the portfolio because it was a great year for stocks? No. We will sell enough of the stocks to get the mix to 65/35.

Suppose stocks fell to 60% of the Target Date Fund at the end the year because the stock market fell? Would that matter? No. In this case, we will sell enough of the bond fund to add to stocks to bring the mix to 65/35.

And, oh by the way, we will do this again every year.

Think about what I just said for a moment. Does it really make sense to fire the people who made you money and give it to the people who didn't do as well or lost your money?!" Because that's what's happening in this case. That's what rebalancing means.

Look at it this way, would you be willing to invest more time with people you know who suck the life out of you, or people whose company you enjoy and who nurture the very best of who you are and who you can become? In this situation, at least, the way the Target Date Fund works is like saying you need to hang out with people who don't add value to your life.

Get the idea? For those of you who understand business, if I came to you and said "I see that you have 80% of your sales and profit coming from 20% of your customers. We need to rebalance that.

Let's tell some of the 20% to go away and devote time, talent and money to try to get the worst customers to pay on time and buy more of your least profitable goods and services even though they are slow pay or end up in collections." If I said that to you I have no doubt you would throw me out of your office as fast as possible. And, you should!

Is the Wall Street meaning of rebalancing clearer now?

In case you missed it, rebalancing is not just confined to the Target Date Funds

26

in your 401(k). More likely than not, it is the driving idea at the core of your 401(k) plan: It's called Modern Portfolio Theory and asset allocation.

So do you want to be in a Target Date Fund? I'll leave that one up to you now that you have a better idea how they work.

xoxoxo

Target Date Funds - Continued

I've been looking forward to bringing this Episode to you because today we're going to circle back to one of our earlier topics... The Target Date Fund. I came across this information several months ago, which was new to me, and I think it's important for you to know.

Recall the Target Date fund was a brain child of Wall Street to capture fees on about one-third of the money in 401(k) plans that was just sitting in money market accounts. I have no doubt they were going crazy because they were so close to a huge windfall. Salivating like a chained dog with a juicy bone just out of reach.

Long story short, in 2006 Wall Street finally got Congress to approve Target Date funds as the "default" option for workplace plans.

In the middle of 2012, this product had accumulated over $350 Billion dollars in assets under management. I'm sure Wall Street is Happy.

But here's the thing: Based on a SEC survey, it would seem, 65% of investors either weren't sure or actually believed these funds would guarantee them income in retirement.

In truth these funds don't guarantee anything, not a specific annual return, no safety of principal and no guarantee against losses.

In THEORY, they are supposed to regularly change up the investment mix so that as you approach and enter retirement your total portfolio will be less risky, if for no other reason than as you get older, you simply don't have the time to make up for catastrophic losses.

But here's the point of this discussion... If Target Date Funds are supposed to be the answer for those of you who are unwilling or unable to choose from the investments in your 401(k) plan, isn't it reasonable to believe that Wall Street figured out the formula?

27

Apparently not. There are two articles which appeared in June 2012. The first was in Forbes: titled "Should You Trust Your Retirement To A Target Date Fund?" And the second was in The New York Times: titled "Target-Date Funds Not Equally Safe."

The Times article poses the question for a hypothetical 63 year old. How much of your portfolio should be in the stock market? One Target Date Fund manager says the answer is 63% while another says the first is wrong and the answer is 37%.

That's a pretty wide difference of opinion!

But it is what it is. In the example given one 2015 Target Date Mutual Fund would have 63% of your portfolio in bond FUNDs and the other would have 63% of your portfolio in the Stock Market?

While most investors have no idea there could possibly be such a huge difference in funds of the same date, once they are aware, what then? It seems the fund with the heavy bond allocation is trying to avoid stock market losses which is arguably a valid goal. Yet, the fund with the heavy stock allocation is focused on the fund owner not running out of money during a 30 year retirement. Again, not outliving your money is important too.

So what's the answer? Perhaps the better question is "Are you serious?!"

You guys convinced Congress it was in my best interest to push me into an investment (granted I can opt-out) because I was unable or unwilling to make a choice. You didn't have a universal plan to manage my money; and, now I get to either trust you, or, I'm back to having to choose for myself all over again. Tell me again how this is helping me?

I mean what exactly did Wall Street say to Congress to get them to OK this as the "go to" investment. Remember, the way this works is employees are automatically invested in these products unless they opt-out and choose their own investments. So what exactly is this?

In my opinion, what I have said all along, is this is a product created by wall street for wall street to capture fees on billions of dollars which were sitting idle, because creating a product was a revenue generator vs. adding cost and sacrificing profit margins by dedicating the time talent and money to actually educate you so you can make better investment decisions.

If you've ever been to a mandatory employee meeting to educate you on your company 401(k) plan, were you comfortable talking in a group setting about your specific financial situation? Or, does your company just pass out enrollment booklets and expect you to read the material, understand it on your own and fill out the forms? Or are you directed to a website with an overwhelming amount of general information, a calculator and an 800 number to a call center?

How about a personal approach. Face-to-face meetings with employees and their family members if the employee wants another set of eyes and ears to help them? If not face-to-face how about one individual an employee can call, e-mail, text or whatever.

Personal finance is personal. It's not a one size fits all product which is frankly not capable of solving everyone's unique situation and goals for retirement.

If you are in a Target Date Fund, at least look it up on morningstar.com. Find out what the investments are and what they are targeted to be as you get closer to retirement. I've said it before and I'll likely say it again. No one but you and your family is going to experience the financial outcomes of these decisions. You owe it to yourself to learn what you can or find someone you know, like and trust to help you.

xoxoxo

The Future of Target Date Funds

Finally, I wanted to share the explosive growth of Target Date Funds on the main menu of 401(k) investment options.

I saw a recent report which suggests these funds will comprise 68% of 401(k) contributions by 2018. I find this disturbing news however inevitable it may be.

Why inevitable? Well, The bulk of money going into this product is the result of the Pension Protection Act of 2006, which allows **employers** to **automatically** enroll eligible employees in their 401(k) plans **and** direct the participants' contributions to target date funds.

While it is not being marketed this way, Employers are forcing a solution. What made me angry was a statement in the report claiming target date funds are the preferred choice among young people. That's like saying rat meat was the preferred choice of prisoners' of war when it was the only source of daily protein to be found in POW camps. You could choose not to eat it; but, to say it was a preferred choice... please...

Employers following the rules of the the Pension Protection Act skirt the issue by allowing participants to opt-out of these investments; but, the fundamental issue has always been there's historically been a population of participants who are unwilling or unable to make an investment decision. How would you grade your Plan Provider's investment education?

I think the other reason this trend is inevitable has to do with human psychology. In marketing, it's called social proof. People tend to feel more comfortable with decisions if many other's before them have also made the same decision even though it's no guarantee the same choice works for everyone.

I believe this could ultimately result in an effect known to skilled negotiators referred to as the Winner's curse. The Winner's curse happens when an offer is immediately accepted by the other party during negotiations. The term implies that although the offer was accepted, the person making the offer failed to get as good a deal as possible. I believe Target Date Funds could be a Winner's curse not only for employees but for employers as well. because employers accepted the first offer by plan providers to solve the problem of poor education.

Anyway, enough of my rant, it just get's my blood boiling when I see marketing like this cleverly disguised as news.

xoxoxo

The Secret Formula that (nearly) Destroyed Your 401(k)

At this point, we're going to talk about Asset Allocation Strategies and how your plan provider (and Wall Street in general) hopes you invest your 401(k) portfolio.

Before we really get started, let's back up a moment to get a better perspective.

This investment philosophy or theory began in the academic world, with what is called "Modern Portfolio Theory" or MPT. The goal of this academic theory is quite simple: create a portfolio that will give you the greatest return on your investment with the lowest possible risk through diversification; and, then, deliver the result in an easy to consume format.

How do you know your 401(k) is using Modern Portfolio Theory?

Answer: the easy to consume format is the pie-chart.

If you are instructed to answer a number of questions about your risk tolerance and the output is a pie-chart, you have entered the twilight zone, MPT. Don't get me wrong, I am a firm believer in diversification. Diversification simply means don't put all your eggs in one basket. However, the way Wall Street has sold this theory is as a packaged product which consumers understand as an event not a process.

So, back to the academic theory: It's important to understand just how this model is constructed so you can make a clearer choice on how to use it. The model begins by collecting historical data around different types of investments.

Without numbing your brain with statistical sampling theory, the idea here was to try to understand the history of investment returns AND just how extreme the results have been over time AND how one particular investment may behave compared to one or more other investment choices.

For example: assuming the average return for stocks, based on data collected, is 10% but the extremes range from gains of 30% to losses of 50%, the spread between the 30% number and the 50% number, is called a statistical "variance." The researchers then looked at the returns and measured how stock returns moved, say compared to bond returns. This measure was defined by researchers as "correlation."

Put another way, they gathered the historical data around how stocks moved vs. how bonds moved. If they moved in the same direction, they were identified as having a "positive" correlation. If they moved in opposite directions, they were identified as having a "negative" correlation.

Some people believe that Gold has a negative correlation vs. stocks. In other words, if stocks in general are falling, they believe the price of Gold will rise. Got the idea?

Ok. So researchers compiled massive amounts of data points on particular investments to include returns, correlations, and variances observed over 50 to 75 years or for as long as these data points had been reported.

We are talking about a mountain of data here and the challenge for researchers was to compress the data to make it useful.

So they took each particular investment and created what they then called "stationary" data points for each of the inputs. What is a stationary data point?

You would recognize it as an average. Let's take a string of numbers: 33, 28, 21, -9, -12, -22, 28, 11, 5 and 16. The calculated AVERAGE is 9.9. Interestingly, this string of numbers is the return for Large Cap Stocks observed from 1997 to 2006.

So for purposes of modeling, MPT would assume that the relevant, stationary data point for Large Cap Stock returns would be, in this case, 9.9%. The fact that this "return" never actually happened even once over the period is ignored. To save you the trouble here are the numbers once more: 33, 28, 21, -9, -12, -22, 28, 11, 5 and 16.

I won't numb your brain with the computation of the "stationary" variance or correlation numbers; because I think you get the idea.

The relevant point is while this is all interesting from an academic point of view, the question is how useful is this as a predictor of the future?

To an investor who assumes Asset Allocation can actually predict what will happen in his or her portfolio over the next 10 or 20 years, may I suggest you simply look at the returns presented in your first pie-chart and see if you actually experienced those returns.

The unmentioned assumption in MPT is that the future will consistently behave in the same fashion as these stationary inputs.

Never mind that this has never happened.

The most recent source of criticism of Modern Portfolio Theory was the grinding market losses of 2008. One of the implicit assumptions of MPT has to do with correlations.

Specifically, it is assumed that the correlation between asset classes is constant.

Let's go back a moment. Correlation simply measures the degree one asset class follows another. Correlations can range from +1.0 (assets have returns that move in lockstep together) to -1.0, (assets have mirror opposite returns).

To say the correlation between Large Cap Stocks and Small Cap Stocks is 0.72

or 72% simply means that Small Cap Stocks will go up 72 cents for every dollar increase in Large Cap Stocks.

During the grinding market losses of 2008, EVERYTHING became correlated.

EVERYTHING lost money.

In other words historical correlations proved invalid. Even asset classes which had a negative correlation, HISTORICALLY (the theory being if one asset class went down a negatively correlated asset would go up) turned on their heels and became positively correlated.

What experience tells us is that at the very time MPT is SUPPOSED to protect our portfolios, the THEORY falls apart.

For a little homespun wisdom, as Yogi Berra said, "In theory, there is no difference between theory and practice. In practice, there is."

The takeaway for 401(k) investors is while diversification is a prudent investment strategy, asset allocation as a static, never to be changed formula is not prudent.

Asset Allocation is a process not an event.

Average Statistical Relationships applied to your portfolio are not likely to help over the next 10 or 20 years.

Solution: Tactical Asset Allocation, measuring what is and adjusting portfolio investments accordingly, vs. trying to use 50 to 75 years of data points to predict what will happen over the next 10 or 20 years, just makes more sense.

xoxoxo

How to cure Asset Allocation Anguish

Actually answering the genuine questions of Plan Participants is a good reminder for me that not everyone knows what I've learned over 30 plus years in the investment industry.

The Participant had asked for a ranking of the investment options in his plan off the 401(k) Owners Manual Website. And, studying the proprietary rankings and our discussion around the benefit of choosing the top three funds, his first question centered around if he needed a more diversified mix in his portfolio because there were no international funds or bond funds ranked in the top three funds.

So, I thought it may be helpful to address the diversification issue. Here's the thing, diversification is commonly confused with Asset Allocation because the terms are used interchangeably in the industry. Shame on us. We assume you know what we're talking about.

As we just discussed, Asset Allocation is a theory which supposes risk of loss can be managed by spreading investments over a broad range of different assets. It's also known as Modern Portfolio Theory. The theory being not all asset values will move in the same direction at the same time. For example, The theory suggests that if stock values are falling, bond prices are stable or rising; or, if US stocks are falling, there are international stock markets which will be stable or rising.

Perhaps the most commonly understood fund model is the target date fund. Again, the theory being you can protect your investment by annually changing the portfolio mix to include a lesser proportion of stock investments.

The most complex models spread the assets between stocks (both domestic and international), bonds (again both domestic and international), commodities, real estate, foreign currencies and the list can get as long as there are asset classes to fill the pie. This is usually the model used by 401(k) providers.

But, ask yourself. Did this work for you in 2008? I imagine it did not because ALL asset classes fell, and they ALL fell at the same time. The asset allocation theory failed at the very time the theory said it was supposed to work. However, the mutual fund industry, the 401(k) industry and the investment industry in general have stubbornly held on to this theory. And, they continue spending massive amounts of advertising dollars to continue promoting it.

Let's move on to Diversification. Diversification on the other hand is the simple idea that you don't put all your eggs in one basket.

You spread the risk so that if one investment loses value you don't lose everything. In the case of the three funds we were looking with this listener: T. Rowe Price New Horizons holds approximately 213 stocks; T. Rowe Price Mid-Cap Growth holds approx. 136 stocks; and, Goldman Sachs Mid Cap Value holds approximately 111 stocks.

Clearly, if the fund managers make a mistake and one of the stocks they bought goes out of business, the entire portfolio is not destroyed. This is what diversification means. It's really that simple.

As far as international funds or bond funds are concerned, the rankings (which is really no more than measuring the market) will tell us when these assets are showing strength and we can reposition the portfolio to get in front of that strength.

More importantly, because we use a substitute for cash along with the S&P 500 index, we will see how the stock index is moving in relation to the other investments offered as well as cash.

When the markets begin to falter, as they did in early 2008, the ranking for cash will rise and there will be time to reposition the portfolio. Remember, cash is an investment alternative. Wall Street doesn't want you to be aware of that fact.

The next issue raised by the Participant was "Picking the proper funds and what percentage to put in each fund is the question that I struggle with the most."

I assured him, You are not alone. The rankings will keep you in the "proper" funds for as long as they are demonstrating relative strength, and no longer.

As far as the percentage to put in each fund. Here is my thinking.

Diversification risk is actually solved when you buy one fund. Long ago I saw a study which suggested once you get beyond fifteen stocks in a portfolio there is a diminishing return for further diversification.

While that may be the case for individuals buying individual stocks, it's not the norm for mutual fund portfolios and that's ok. Looking at the funds we mentioned, the "least" diversified held 111 stocks.

By using three funds what you are doing is all you can reasonably do to manage the risk(s) at the fund management level. You are diversifying the fund management risks.

One fund management risk is the age and experience of the portfolio manager.

Some funds have built a reputation and following because of a super-star manager: Fidelity's Peter Lynch or Legg Mason's Bill Miller come to mind. The risk is what happens to the performance of those funds if they step down?

Fund manager changes are not generally made known to the public at large. Industry professionals, or some at least, keep track of this information. By the way, performance usually does suffer with a portfolio manager change.

"Style drift" is another fund management risk.

Suppose your asset allocation model says you need some percentage of "Mid-cap Growth" stocks in your portfolio. You look to the choice in your 401(k), see one that is described as a Mid-cap Growth Fund and you say super. Done and done.

But, sometimes, portfolio managers start dipping into stocks outside that mandate because they are chasing what they think is a promising area. In this example they may start dipping into small cap growth or micro-cap growth stocks because that segment of the market suddenly becomes hot. Unless you monitor in detail what they are buying, you would likely miss this distinction.

Those are just a few of the fund management risks investors face, usually without knowing it.

In my opinion, spending the time to fine tune an exact percentage for each fund isn't worth the effort. Like the diminishing returns issue we discussed around over diversification, I believe, three funds, giving each one-third is fine. Why?

Because the rankings will do the heavy lifting to manage these risks. Measuring the market and rankings will pick up on any significant problems at the fund management level. It will show up in the performance numbers and hence the rankings.

So, in my opinion, there is no reason to struggle with picking the right funds and what percentage to invest in each. The rankings will get you there and keep you there for as long as they are performing, and no longer.

xoxoxo

Steal this 401(k) Tip

Ready? Today I want to give you something quick and easy you can use right away... and for the rest of your life. The secret is this: Focus more on less.

Studies have found having too many choices will interfere with the ability to make a decision. That's rather a strange reality, particularly today when almost any information is readily available online. However, it does make sense when you think about it.

Indecision, confusion and inaction are not uncommon especially when there is so much information. Limited to three or four choices, most decisions are not very hard. Increasing the number to 20 or 40 or a thousand or more and the decision-making process has to change. The focus by necessity becomes not so much what's best as how do I filter out choices so I can make a decision.

I remember talking with a retired Human Resources professional who worked with a division of General Electric. He was telling me about their hiring process. He said after they published a Want Ad for a professional job, they would typically not even check the PO Box for three or four weeks.

Once they finally collected the responses, they would gather in a conference room and rip through the letters and resumes with the expressed purpose of disqualifying the applicant. He said they normally spent ten to sixty seconds on each one! The idea was to take thousands of responses and try to pair down the population to about ten.

As an aside, his suggestion for people responding to job listings was this: look for ads that are several months old and respond as if they were just published. He said: first, you will be compared to the top ten candidates already selected; and, second, they will likely spend three to five minutes on your resume vs. the ten to sixty seconds mentioned earlier.

Back to your 401(k): As I recall, the average number of choices in most 401(k) plans is about seventeen to twenty, including Target Date Funds. You do not have a say in how many choices you have in your 401(k) investment line-up. But, you can limit those choices quite easily.

The filter I use for people who pay for my service usually goes like this:

First I eliminate all Target Date Funds and make two additions to the population: the S&P 500 Index and a money market option. Then I study the current relative strength rankings of that universe. The final filter is to look at the individual point and figure charts for each. If you've never heard of that type of chart, you can check them out online, for free, at StockCharts.com. We'll cover, in depth, how to use this in PART SEVEN of the book.

Again: Focus more on less. Whether you are trying to make an investment decision or a decision about anything in your life. Remember this, do not spend all your time trying to evaluate every possible detail of every possible option. Adopt a logical, organized systematic process to make a decision and then make a decision.

Also don't get caught in the mind-set that once you make a decision you will have to live with it forever. You are allowed to make new decisions when you get new information. It does not mean your previous decision was wrong.

xoxoxo

A Word On Company Stock

Some of you may have the choice to buy stock in your company. It may be offered inside or outside your 401(k). What I would suggest, as a general guideline, is to limit the ownership of stock in your employer to no more than ten percent of your total net worth.

The decision to buy stock in your employer, in a perfect world, should be motivated by profit potential rather than yielding to real or imagined pressure to be a team player or create the perception of employee confidence to potential investors outside the company.

The tools to be discussed later, will guide you to objectively evaluate such an investment. Remember, you are likely dependent on your employer for your current income. Does it really make sense to overweight your investments and the success of your retirement on the prospects of a single business? To do so would violate one of the first rules of successful investing which is diversification.

Diversification simply states you should not put all your eggs in one basket. It is the first rule of risk management. Think of what happened to the employees of Enron who got caught up in the enthusiasm… only to lose everything.

xoxoxo

The Self-directed Brokerage Option

Each Plan Provider (the company that provides the 401(k) investment platform to your company for your benefit) may call it something a little different –

TD Ameritrade calls it a Self Directed Brokerage Account;

JP Morgan Chase Investment Services calls it their Retirement Brokerage Services Self-Directed Account;

Fidelity through their Institutional Retirement Services Company simply calls it BrokerageLink;

Charles Schwab calls it their Personal Choice Retirement Account or PCRA;

Obviously, there are many other plan providers and you will just have to look through your plan documents to see if your company adopted a self-directed option and what they call it.

Anyway, this feature will allow you to "journal" monies off the main menu into a sub-account within your 401(k).

Once in this area you are free to choose for yourself where you want to invest. Again, every plan is different and you will have to find out what choices you have. I have seen this option limited to a list of 1,400 more mutual funds; and, other plans where you are free to invest in most anything you can buy in an Individual Retirement Account.

A bit of perspective before we go further. This choice is relatively new to 401(k) plans. It was created with the passage of a new law called The Pension Protection Act of 2006 which became effective in January of 2008. The spirit of the law was to level the playing field for employees. In other words, it was to allow employees to be free from the limited investment choices offered by Plan Providers.

It also made provision for employees to be able to pay for independent investment advice with pre-tax money from their own 401(k) account balances. In compliance with the law, a number of Plan Providers have established policies and procedures for employees to pay for advice from professionals who are unaffiliated with the Plan Provider. Included among such firms are Fidelity and Schwab, to name a few.

If you want to know if this is allowed under your own plan, you will likely have to ask someone in Human Resources. In my experience, this is not a plan feature which is common knowledge among employees or even members of the Human Resources Department. So, the first answer you get from HR may not be correct. Ask for a Plan Document called the Summary Plan Description and look for yourself.

If someone in your Human Resources Department tells you this is illegal, I assure you, it is not.

Chapter Four
The Plan Provider & Your Company

In this section, we'll be addressing the secret and not so secret roles which are played by Plan Providers and the Companies which hire them to provide your 401(k) retirement plan. Again, the benefit for you is to be aware of what is at stake so you can take steps to make the most of your 401(k) plan.

xoxoxo

The Secrets of the 401(k) Industry

I recently came across a white paper on the Internet titled *The Secrets of the 401(k) Industry* by Edward "Ted" Siedle. Ted began his career in law with the SEC's division of investment management, which regulates money managers and mutual funds. Later he was legal counsel, director of compliance to Putnam investments. He has testified before the Senate Banking Committee regarding the mutual fund scandals (in 2002?) and as an expert in various Madoff and other litigations. Which, I assume means, any number of times, he has been formally recognized as an expert witness by a court of law.

He has appeared on CNN, Fox Business, CNBC, and Bloomberg News and is a regular contributor to Forbes magazine. I think we can assume he is an authority.

Let's see if I can put his report in perspective, to make this relevant for you.

The secrets of the 401(k) industry begins with identifying the economic self interest of the players in this drama. First up are employers, your company, also known as the plan sponsor. The next Player is the plan provider, the business which sold the 401(k) platform to your employer. And finally you, the employee, also known in the industry jargon as the plan participant. Okay?

Quickly then:
1. Employers equal plan sponsors,
2. Financial firms equal plan providers, and,

3. You equal the plan participant.

The main plot is that while all the investment risk and, yes, most all of the cost of 401(k) plans rest with you, the investment results, in large part, depend upon the Provider chosen for you. In turn, what investments they recommend to your employer which end up as the choices you have in your 401(k) plan influence the investment results.

I know that was a mouthful - I'll see if I can make it easier to swallow.

You are powerless to select what investment options are available in your plan even though you are mostly paying the bill and your chances of building a large enough nest egg for retirement, or not, depends on the investments offered in your plan.

The important point here is whatever investments you buy, sell or hold from inside your plan will either achieve the retirement goal, or not. No one but you will experience the outcome. Okay?

Back to Ted's report, "...and while employers are generally more knowledgeable than you in these matters, an overwhelming majority of employers have relied on providers for turnkey solutions." In other words, it's easier for your employer to say "yes" to anything the financial firm recommends.

Why is that? Because by design, employers have no liability, no obligation, to ensure that your 401(k) actually can accumulate enough money to support you in retirement; and, therefore, employers have little incentive to police what providers are actually doing.

Clearly employers have an economic interest in providing 401(k) plans because they are effective in attracting and retaining talented employees needed to build their business. Ted quotes a study however in which 87% of employers confidentially stated they do not believe 401(k) plans will be able to deliver the implied benefits.

To paraphrase Ted: of all the parties involved with 401(k) plans you, the participant, are the least knowledgeable regarding the complex, mostly hidden, practices of the investment industry. And it is unreasonable to expect that you will, in all your spare time, working 40 to 60 hours a week, somehow acquired the expertise to skillfully sift through all the investment alternatives bundled for you by providers, even though it's your money at risk.

So what we have is a system where, shall we say, disinterested employers are choosing 401(k) vendors, with their own profit motive, to provide a product for employees who will bear not only the cost but the performance risk.

I guess the phrase "the fox guarding the hen house" comes to mind because the overwhelming weight of the evidence may suggest providers have exploited their informational advantage over both employers and you. The informational advantage can be maintained for no other reason than neither you nor your employer can commit the time to scrutinize the financial firm's self interest in deciding which investment products will be allowed in your 401(k).

Let's put this another way: the financial firms own the race course. They get to choose which horses will run in the race and the horses they select pay an entry fee. They don't care which horse wins. They make money when you bet on any horse, so long as you do bet. It has not gone unnoticed the financial industry has gone to great lengths to be sure you do by getting the rules changed to make Target Date Funds the default investment option in most plans.

Ted then goes on to discuss the advantages of the old retirement system, the pension plan. Ted details the relative costs of each type of plan pointing out the overwhelmingly higher costs associated with mutual fund product versus the fees pensions pay for institutional money management.

He then goes on to shine a light on all the unscrupulous behaviors of the industry. No surprise to me, although some made me raise an eyebrow. The balance of Ted's white paper goes into detail on how financial firms have gamed the system.

The ultimate question Ted raises is: whose economic interests prevail? As it stands now, it would seem clear, the winner is the financial firms. His conclusion calls for the regulatory overhaul of the 401(k) industry.

 And from my perspective that is a noble objective and one which should be pursued.

Yet you, the participant, don't have years to wait for regulations to be enacted and then bet regulators will be successful on the enforcement front. I know many of you share my frustration around the economic crisis of 2008. Of note is that no one in the financial industry has gone to jail, unlike the Savings & Loan scandal when industry leaders were aggressively pursued, convicted, fined and jailed.

As an aside, I was talking about this very point with a friend of mine and he surprised me only because it seemed so obvious once he said it. He suggested the reason the S&L scandal resulted in fines convictions and jail was because the financial industry pushed the agenda with the goal of crushing a very real competitor, the S&L industry. Perhaps the reason we are not seeing the same vigor today is the financial firms are not going to put themselves in jail. Food for thought.

My goal in bringing this white paper to your attention has been to help you see where you stand in this dynamic. And the answer is, unfortunately, pretty much alone.

However despite the conditions which exist and the games being played behind the scenes, you can have a fighting chance to secure your financial future.

But it will not be handed to you on a silver platter. You will have to step up. It will not happen as fast as you would like. But it will not take as long as you may think. This is doable.

What we've tried to present are the tools to eliminate the unnecessary, all the noise and confusion and mystery, so you can see clearly what is necessary to make intelligent decisions in the limited spare time you have.

xoxoxo

The Letter of the Law

More from Edward "Ted" Siedle, this time from one of the articles he contributed to Forbes magazine. One of my favorite monikers the media has bestowed on Ted is "the Sam Spade of Money Management."

The title of this article is "IBM 401(k) Participants Need Their Own "Shadow" Fiduciary to Guard Retirement Benefits"

The background of the article circles around IBMs decision, beginning in 2013, to change the timing of the company's matching contribution to their employees' 401(k) from semi-monthly to an end of the year lump sum contribution.

To put this in perspective for you, according to BrightScope® which is the leading independent provider of retirement plan ratings and investment analytics, IBM 401(k) Plus Plan currently has over 203,800 active participants and over $37.6 Billion in plan assets.

IBMs announcement apparently plucked some nerves judging from the comments on BrightScope's website.

One person writes: The 401(k) company match modifications, which only pay out at the end of the year on Dec 15 should you still have the honor of being an IBMer, are not meant to encourage good employees to stick around... it's a loophole in the law which "could" save the company huge amounts of money. This savings would be realized when they schedule mass layoffs of US employees in the 4th quarter each year. Insult to injury would be if those pink slips arrive on Dec 14 annually.

Ted's article points out that under applicable federal pension law, employees have no legal right to participate in the administrative and investment decisions of the of the plan.

Overall Plan decisions are generally left up to the employer. Decisions like matching contributions, if any, the investments offered in the plan (like company stock, mutual funds, guaranteed investment contracts, a self-directed brokerage window and what's available through the brokerage window, like direct investment in bonds, stocks and exchange traded funds) are generally up to the employer.

In addition, the employer generally gets to decide when and how employees are allowed to borrow money from their own account balances as well as whether or not employees can use pre-tax money from their own account to hire independent financial advisors who are not affiliated with the plan.

According to Ted the existing legal framework has been failing participants for decades. He states "The rules have worked out just swimmingly for sponsors of retirement plans and the financial services firms skimming from such plans."

I only just made the connection recently that the Pension Protection Act of 2006 which came into effect in Jan. of 2008 was actually a win for financial services firms.

I thought the provisions were heavily slanted toward leveling the playing field in favor of employees; but, apparently there was included a provision to allow Employers to make Target Date Funds the default investment vs. money market funds.

Since the Law became effective, Target Date Fund assets under management have exploded to over $3 Billion Dollars. And, yes. financial services firms get to collect higher fees than they did on money market accounts.

Anyway, Ted suggests some out-of-the-box thinking for IBM employees. Specifically to establish their own "Shadow" 401(k) fiduciary or guardian to represent their interests alone.

While this guardian organization he proposes will not have any legal authority, it may serve to keep the company on the defensive by keeping employees educated and perhaps thwart further efforts to weaken the 401(k).

His suggestion is they establish an on-line presence in the hopes of advocating for regulatory changes by targeting legislators and regulators.

While I agree this is a worthwhile endeavor, older employees, with only 15 years to retirement, may not have the time to benefit from the effort. Paraphrasing Ted: Employers, with infinite resources, assisted by expert advisors, and limited incentive to tell the truth, pursue their own objectives whilst workers are kept in the dark.

My own suggestion to employees is to use the tools we discuss here to see for yourself what the markets are telling you. Remember, you do not have to be invested at all times and in all markets. Smart people have known for centuries the secret to accumulating wealth is avoiding catastrophic losses.

xoxoxo

But You Are Not Helpless

AOL, without any fanfare, made a significant change to their 401(k) plan. It was identical to the move IBM made which we just discussed. However, the outcome was different.

AOL's employees didn't see it coming. The company, like IBM before it, decided to change the way they match employees' contributions to their 401(k). Rather than matching contributions every pay period, they decided they could save money by only making their contribution, in a lump sum, at the end of the year. The point being, if you're not employed at the end of the year, effectively, you wouldn't get a matching contribution.

However, given the power of social media, employees found out about the change and a firestorm started. In response, the Chairman and CEO held a town-hall meeting with all 5,000 employees and tried to blame the change on

ObamaCare and singled out two woman who had "distressed babies" causing AOL to pay $2 million "above and beyond" necessary medical expenses.

"Distressed babies" became a flash-point, blaming women and babies was really poor salesmanship. And, it didn't go unnoticed the Chairman's compensation nearly quadrupled in 2012 to $12.1 million, from $3.2 million in 2011.

After a week of really bad negative publicity, the Chairman reversed his 401(k) decision and offered an apology for his earlier comments. Which may suggest the move to change the 401(k) was driven by a profit motive vs. a necessary cost cutting move. Not a good day for the AOL leader.

What's the lesson for you? Pay attention to what's happening with your 401(k) and don't be afraid to use your voice. Without the publicity caused by Social Media and employees voicing their concerns, it's questionable whether or not the Chairman would have reversed the decision. Remember, having access to tools, like Social Media in this case, doesn't do any good if you don't actually use them.

So what's the point? What's this have to do with your 401(k)?

Here's the thing...

It was not so very long ago, people would have never questioned the change AOL attempted. If they did, it may have been a few employees commiserating over the water-cooler or at lunch. But, their voice would have barely registered as a whisper.

That's changed. Today there are tools, literally at your fingertips, which were just not widespread even 10 years ago. Technology is now making easy, what was once very difficult or simply impossible for the average individual.

The challenge is having the willingness to pick up those tools today.

xoxoxo

Plan Providers Play to the Status Quo

Plan Providers, the financial companies who are in the business of providing the 401(k) platform for your company, have subtile ways to influence public opinion and your company.

There was an article that caught my eye on March 12th 2013, titled "Is

Groupthink hurting your 401(k)" which was on the MarketWatch blog.

The thrust of the article was based on a research report by non-other than the Vanguard Group. Vanguard is one of the largest Plan Providers in the market.

The researchers suggested there may be problems with your company's investment committee. Let me explain, larger companies which have 401(k) plans may have an in-house committee who's job it is to oversee the plan and interact with the financial services company which your company hired to give you the 401(k) platform.

The duties of the company's investment committee may include:

1. approving the investment choices available in your plan,
2. deciding if and to what extent the company will match your contributions,
3. the timing of company matching contributions,
4. if the plan allows participants to borrow money from their own account,
5. if the plan will allow for a self-directed brokerage sub-account and what investments are to be allowed through that channel and,
6. if plan participants will be allowed to use money from their retirement account to pay for financial advisory service outside the plan.

The article suggests the Vanguard researchers identified some recurring Committee problems such as: Chasing Performance; Groupthink; Inexperience; and, oversized committees.

Vanguard found committees spend just over half their time looking over past performance of various investments. They cited another of their own studies to suggest committees which chase "hot" mutual funds in place of lagging funds can get the timing wrong where the "hot" funds are at the end of a winning streak and the laggards are beginning a come-back.

Following the link cited in the article to Vanguard's research: Vanguard suggested committees should spend time on Costs; Asset Allocation; Portfolio Construction; Spending; Liability Management; Transparency; Due Diligence; and Risk. They further suggested committees spend less time on Manager Changes, Evaluating Investment Strategies; Manager Performance; and, monitoring Financial Markets.

It seems a clear conflict of interest to me that Vanguard would be recommending how committees spend their time to fulfill their fiduciary obligation to employees. Suggesting members spend less time Evaluating

Investment Strategies; Manager Performance; and Manager Changes is, it seems to me, in the financial self-interest of Vanguard rather than employees.

The next recurring Committee problem cited in the report was Groupthink or "confirmation bias." The issue being strong willed, persuasive committee members coming to meetings prepared, according to Vanguard, with opinion vs. facts. And, in the process, these members tend to seek out arguments and evidence to back up their opinions rather than sift through evidence objectively. I wonder how Vanguard's own interests and opinions are challenged by alleged strong willed, prepared, persuasive committee members.

The next recurring committee problem cited has to do with too many members. Vanguards sweet spot seems to be between six and ten. Over ten, committees become unwilling and inefficient. Again, the question comes to mind unwilling and inefficient for Vanguard?

And finally the recurring problem cited in the article is inexperience with about half the committee members in their survey having five years or less tenure on the committee, suggesting these green members may be less likely to value Vanguard's findings.

The point here is you have a popular financial media outlet, MarketWatch dot com, reporting this so called research as news, for whose benefit? Is this news to promote the financial interests of Vanguard or the well being of employees?

Personally, I see no problem with strong willed, prepared, persuasive committee members representing employee interests. I see no problem with committee members spending as much time as they feel necessary Evaluating Manager Changes, Investment Strategies; Manager Performance; and, monitoring Financial Markets. I believe these committees are supposed to be concerned with performance as well as negotiating the lowest possible fees for their employees.

And, as far as Vanguard's concern about committee tenure less than five years. I think anyone willing to commit their time and talent to serve on such a committee and who demonstrates the willingness to continue their education around financial investment issues IS perfectly qualified. The last thing you want are a bunch of committee members who are simply "Yes" men (sorry ladies) agreeing with everything Vanguard or any other 401(k) vendor has to say.

What I got from the article is Vanguard is trying to manage Vanguard's

49

business far more than worrying about committees being counterproductive and falling down in the service of employees.

So what can you do?

Have a friendly conversation with your Human Resources contact responsible for the company 401(k). Be gentle with them, ok?

If you mention nothing else, let them know you are concerned about the fees you pay to the mutual funds in your plan. The fees you pay, however small they may seem, over your career, will have a significant impact on the dollar amount you end up with when you retire. It could be $100s of thousands of dollars different. If you don't know what fees are being invisibly deducted from your account, ask; or, ask HR where to find them. You can't control the the direction of the investment markets which will drive most of the performance of your funds; but. you can be sure the funds being used in your plan are low cost.

The lowest cost investment options would be Exchange Traded Funds, ETFs. However, you'll not likely see them on the main menu of investment choices in most plans. Do some research on your own around the fees for ETFs vs. even index mutual funds.

If this makes sense to you, tell Human Resources you would like your company to have a self directed brokerage account adopted for your plan specifically allowing for the purchase of Exchange Traded Funds.

While your at it, tell them too you would like your plan to adopt the provision to allow you to pay for an advisor of your own choosing, unrelated to the financial service company supplying the 401(k) platform, using your own, pre-tax, 401(k) money, directly out of your 401(k) account.

The Pension Protection Act of 2006 talks about this very provision and a number of high profile 401(k) vendors, including Fidelity, already have procedures in place to process such payments; but, only in plans where the companies sponsoring the plans insisted the provision be adopted, over the objection, I'm sure, of the vendors of the plan. In other words, the investment committees demanded these changes.

If you do nothing else, find out who is on the committee in your company and shoot them an e-mail, just to thank them for their service, send a copy to Human Resources. Let them know you appreciate what they're doing. Give them a human face to think about the next time they're representing employee interests at a 401(k) investment committee meeting. Make it personal for them.

Hidden Transfer of Risk to the Plan Participant

How should you define investment risk?

This is more than a theoretical question because how the answer has been framed for you by the investment industry will continue to have an impact on your wealth, in particular your wealth on the day you retire.

Let's stop for a moment to put this in perspective for you by posing the question "How much would you need to invest today to generate expected income of $100,000 this year?"

It's an important question because it's the question you will have to answer once you enter the retirement phase of your life when you wish to give up working day to day for a paycheck. Remember, this is a hypothetical so don't let the answer frighten you.

Take note, the assumption here is: it's reasonable to look for "safe" investments during the retirement years because you are not likely to be adding to your wealth and market losses will reduce the money you will have for day-to-day living expenses.

So, let's look at an investment in a 2 year US Treasury Note in July of 2005: to create a $100,000 return, you would have needed about $2.5 million. Fast forward to July 2012 and you would have needed $45 million to generate the same $100,000 income.

Why? Because of the drop in interest rates from 2005 to 2012. Will rates be this low when you retire? No one knows. And, by the way, don't panic, there are other investment combinations to get you to a $100,000 income which don't require anything close to $45 million dollars.

So let's go back to our discussion of risk. Are you focused on the risk of accumulating too little money for retirement or are you focused on the risk of managing historic volatility? In fairness, it's a trick question because if your 401(k) encourages you to fill out a "risk tolerance" questionnaire and then uses the results to generate a pie-chart, without your expressed consent, you are being led to manage volatility not retirement outcomes.

While we use the terms risk and volatility interchangeably, they are not the same thing. In this case, you would do well to think of risk as the possibility of not having enough money on the day you retire to maintain your desired standard of living for the next thirty years.

Volatility, on the other hand, simply measures the bumpiness of the ride to your retirement date.

xoxoxo

What's "Fair" for Plan Participants

Let's address two relevant issues for employees: Savings rates and restrictions on changing investment selections offered in your plan.

Earlier we talked about the fact that of all the main characters at the 401(k) administrative meeting. Your seat is empty even though it's your wedding we are planning. Imagine a bride who hasn't struggled with a wedding. Think of all the details: the guest list, money, religion, decorations, selection of bridesmaids and groomsmen just to name a few.

Yet, when it comes to planning the structure and options of your 401(k) plan, you are not invited to the party. Your interests are supposed to be represented by your employer and the financial services firm providing the platform. However, the combined economic interests of these two parties may overwhelm your economic best interest.

Case in point: I recently came across a discussion on the Kiplinger website titled "Automatic 401(k) Saving Features No Fail-Safe to Retirement Success"

It was a good overview of the trend in the 401(k) space centered on Auto-enrollment features being adopted by companies at the urging of plan providers. The author noted that the majority of plans, seven out of ten, set the default savings rate at 3% or less.

If you define retirement "success" as being a 401(k) portfolio, in combination with Social Security Benefits, which is supposed to replace 80% of preretirement income, then the 3% default savings rate is not going to get the job done. The article goes on to offer a number of suggestions as to why the rate is so low.

By the way, many experts suggest combined employee and employer contributions should be in the area of twelve to fifteen percent.

Fortunately, you are among the smart ones who have realized auto-pilot hasn't been working and are preparing to grab the wheel if you haven't already.

So I thought it would also be helpful to draw your attention to some roadblocks which have been placed in your path. Roadblocks which are in place to keep you invested at all times and in all markets because it is in the economic interest of the plan provider. The spin they use to justify these restrictions on your ability to manage your investments, of course, is they are trying to protect you.

What I am talking about specifically is plan provisions at the investment level which restrict your ability to buy back into investments you owned for a time and then sold.

One plan I've looked at has a 60 day lock-out for particular funds offered on the main menu of investment options. In other words, if you sell any of the fund, they will not allow you to buy the fund back for a period of 60 days. You are locked out. I've seen some that extend the lock out to 90 days, And, still another has rather a scary warning - a threat to your employment!

This particular plan devotes three pages of its 401(k) Investment Guide Handbook describing the restrictions and consequences of changing your investments mandated not only by the employer but by the financial services company the employer hired to provide the plan platform.

The rational given is fairness. In other words, they suggest it's not fair to "long-term" shareholders. They claim moving in and out of investments disrupts the efficient management of the fund portfolio, increases brokerage costs and administrative costs for the particular fund.

Personally, I find the rational laughable because the financial firm hired to provide this plan is one of the largest providers out there; this particular 401(k) plan itself has over $5 billion of employee money; and, the individual funds being offered on the main menu each manage so much money they cannot possibly be influenced by, let alone dominated by, any individual or group of plan participants acting together.

To me, it seems just a cleverly disguised attempt to keep the sheep in line. Consequences for violating this plan's restrictions range from a single-fund block to a complex-wide block to disciplinary action up to and including termination of employment.

53

But, it is what it is. The point here is you need to look at your plan description to root out the restrictions (however paranoid or self-serving they may be) and just make a note of them. You would also do well to check your savings rate. Remember, savings will have the greatest impact on a successful retirement outcome.

xoxoxo

Company Communications

Wouldn't it be nice if someone would just tell you which 401(k) investments to choose and give you a heads-up before the market tanked like it did in 2008?

Some time ago I checked my mail box. You know, the United States Postal Service mail. As I was sorting through the ones to go right into the trash, I saw one piece I thought I should open based on the return address. But, when I looked closer, it was addressed to George Huss... or Current Resident.

I just started laughing. I don't know how much this company spends on direct mail; but, in an attempt, I guess, to be sure they don't waste any money, they put this catch-all phrase "or current resident" on the envelope.

Think about it. Going to all the trouble to craft a message for a particular audience and then hoping to get someone to open the letter, you start with the resident's name. I don't think I'm unique because I expect mail to be personal and relevant to me. Once I saw the phrase "or current resident" I mentally moved it into the junk mail category.

I am amazed marketing experts still do this because the message this sends is we didn't think enough of you to be sure you still live at the address we have. So, oh by the way, it's good enough for a "current resident."

Frankly, We're all too busy and are too distracted to look at anything but what is personal and relevant to us. We unconsciously create filters to help us manage the flood of information coming at us all day long.

The point here is how relevant is the information you get from your 401(k) plan provider?

Do you open their mail or e-mails. Is it generic or specific and personal? Or is it a sales pitch for a fund in your investment line-up they want you to buy? Lately, I've been seeing this kind of marketing material in the mail. The plan provider

54

is promoting the "benefits" of international investing and why this or that fund is great for investors.

What the material doesn't point out is this asset class, international funds, is one of the most expensive in terms of investment management fees. And, while investment returns on non-US investments can be dramatic, so can losses.

What about communications you get from your provider? Are they relevant? I assume the account statements are. At least they tell you the value of what you have in the account. They should also breakdown the values by investment and unrealized gains and losses. So, it is personal and relevant; but, does it tell you what investments are working or if the market is moving in a direction which suggests preservation of capital?

Wouldn't that information be relevant? Wouldn't you like to know the answer to those questions? Why don't they give that to you?

We've gone over the answer earlier. The reason they cannot and will not is ... they don't want responsibility for your investment outcomes. Your company adopted a 401(k) plan to avoid the liability they had under a Pension Plan.

In other words, the Pension Plan forced them to pay you a specific amount of money throughout your retirement regardless of how well they managed the investments. The 401(k) promises you nothing more than a savings and investment platform to allow you to manage your own finances. If you save and invest well, you may have enough money to carry you through your retirement. If you don't, it's not their problem.

However, if they tell you how to invest your money, they fall right back into the liability they were trying to avoid in the first place. So they will never tell you how to invest your money.

So, back to the topic. Be careful when you get Plan/Account Updates from your Plan Provider through your Employer. That "Update" may just be a cleverly disguised sales letter.

xoxoxo
What They Tell You (or Don't) is Important

I remember seeing an illustration and on it was written: "Journalism is printing what someone else does not want printed. Everything else is public relations." It was a quote attributed to George Orwell. As you may imagine by now, I'm a bit of a skeptic, so, I had to do some digging to see if this was actually an Orwell quote.

Interestingly enough, I'm not the first to have asked the question and I found a seemingly authoritative source called quoteinvestigator.com. It looked legit.

Anyway, based on the current data, the site concluded the quote should be labeled anonymous. Which was fine with me. I don't think it makes the quote any less valid.

What was nice was the site also sourced variations on the quote. The most relevant to today's topic was credited to Katharine Graham, the long-time publisher of the Washington Post. She said:

"News is what someone wants suppressed. Everything else is advertising. The power is to set the agenda. What we print and what we don't print matter a lot."

What's the point? What does this have to do with your 401(k)? Think about it. Your plan provider controls the agenda by what they print on your statement and what they do not print on the statement.

This came to mind when I got an email from a listener who had perhaps one too many funds and when we looked at it, we noticed one of the funds had performed better than the S&P 500 index; but significantly below the top two funds offered in the plan.

Well so? Well, while your statement may show performance numbers, what does that really mean to the plan participant. What's the difference between a 74% increase in share value over a two year period vs. a 52% increase over a two year period? Simple math? 22 percent. Yea, so? And that's the point... so.

Suppose your statement had a variance analysis. For those of you who may not know what that is, it's simply how one number differs from what was actually reported vs. what it might have been.

In this case, suppose the participant had $100,000 in the fund with "ONLY" a 52% return over two years. To put the variance in perspective suppose the money had been invested in the fund with the 74 percent return over the two years? The Variance? Twenty-two thousand dollars!

Tell me, what means more to you? That you only got a 52% return or that your account could have been richer by $22,000? Seems like a basic miracle. Put yourself in the better fund and you would be $22,000 richer!

Katharine Graham quote, in my view, applies. "What we print and what we don't print matter a lot."

Let me point out one more illustration. The LA Times reported a story titled: "More U.S. workers are confident of a comfortable retirement"

Now that sounds like great news, yes? If you only read the headline, you'd probably go about your day feeling pretty good. However, the Sub-Headline would take you 180 degrees. It reads: "Eighteen percent of Americans said this year they were very confident about retirement, up from 13% in 2013, a new survey says. But more than a third of respondents had saved less than $1,000."

Entirely different feeling and, I would hope, an entirely different reader response. I hope all of you go look at your 401(k) right now.

xoxoxo

The Risk Tolerance Question

What is inconsistent, nondurable and emotionally driven by the latest experience? In the context of your 401(k) or other investments what I've just described is investor "Risk Tolerance" observed by any number of academic researchers in the area of investor psychology.

What does that mean? Well, it means your attitudes around investment risk are dynamic. They're fluid. They change as your experiences change - particularly your most recent experiences. Just experience an investment loss? You are more likely to be more cautious than if you've experienced a run of investment success.

What's the point? Well, most retirement plans begin with what is called a Risk Tolerance Questionnaire because the government says (and I quote) "a broker must have a reasonable basis to believe that an . . . investment strategy . . . is suitable for the particular customer based on the customer's investment profile."

So the industry created the Risk Tolerance Questionnaire as a tool to comply and the result drives the computer model to spit out a pie chart, the asset allocation model that is "personalized" specifically for you.

Or, so they would have you believe. First of all, it's not at all uncommon for the Risk Scale to range from one to ten with ten being the most aggressive or tolerant of risk. So, if your score is a five, your allocation will be exactly the same as every other five, not really "personalized" is it?

Would you believe a pair of slacks with a 34 waist, 32 long was custom tailored specifically for you? Or a Size 6 dress off the rack - would you say it was custom tailored specifically for you? Of course not.

So, don't be lulled into thinking the asset allocation the software spits out is unique to you and your goals and don't be lulled into the idea it will be forever perfect for you.

What I would suggest is asset allocation models based on Modern Portfolio Theory are an imperfect tool. What I would suggest is, if history is any guide, and in financial markets history is the only guide we have, then there are no perfect models which will work at all times and in all markets.

Think of it this way. Have you ever used a dime to tighten a screw when you didn't have a flat-head screwdriver handy? Have you ever used a safety pin in place of a lost button on a skirt?

If you look at the way you deal with common fixes in other areas of your life you may be able to take some lessons to apply to your investment strategies. You use the tools you have at hand; and, later, when you have access to better tools, you use them.

xoxoxo

How You are Viewed by Plan Providers

Here is a snap-shot of how Plan Providers view Participants…

"Schwab shoos $25 billion of client assets out the door as it calls the bluff of employers with lopsided 401(k) contracts"

This was an article which appeared in a trade journal called RIABIZ whose target market and primary audience is Registered Investment Advisors.

Here's the gist of the article. Seven years ago, Schwab was a late starter in the 401(k) business. In order to move up the pecking order quickly, they bought The 401(k) Company from Nationwide Insurance in Columbus, Ohio. The price? $115 million dollars. What they bought was a client base of more than

100 companies with about 400,000 participants with $21.7 billion in plan assets.

To put that in perspective, they paid about $300 for each participant. Remember, businesses don't buy businesses unless they believe there's profit in it. Sure there are fees to be earned providing the 401(k) platform. In the industry it's called Record-keeping. I'll tell you what the real attraction was in just a moment.

Unfortunately for Schwab, what they couldn't have anticipated was the Department of Labor Rules which came after the purchase requiring participant level, fee disclosures. As a result of those disclosures the industry has been seeing pressure to lower those fees. In turn, where Schwab is concerned, it has called into question the ruling reason why they bought the company in the first place.

And here's the point for you. Hidden in plain sight. Industry observers have stated in black and white Schwab's goal (and by extension every plan provider's goal in getting into this business) is clearly trying to use 401(k) participants to build their retail investor base.

We've discussed this before. The end-game goal for all these providers is to get to manage your assets when you retire and roll-over your 401(k) into an IRA, an individual retirement account. Because the profit on the 401(k) business is so thin they have no incentive to provide an ongoing, one-on-one relationship between you and just one of their representatives. That's why your 401(k) questions are directed to an automated response system or to a call center where you get to talk to the next available clerk.

In truth they cannot afford to provide that kind of relationship with you... until you are ready to become a retail client. I'm sure you've seen the online ads offering you up to $1,000 to rollover your 401(k) into some broker's IRA. Why? Because, that's where the real profit potential is. Particularly if they can convince you to buy high commission products.

Schwab's issue with these particular accounts, under the old contracts, is that Schwab's brand shows up nowhere. They don't have access to those employees and the employees don't even know who the plan provider is. So, come rollover time, Schwab is out in the cold. They certainly aren't first in line to bid for your rollover.

This whole discussion circles back to our description of the Pension Protection

Act of 2006. I believe the spirit of the proposed legislation was an attempt to level the playing field. To allow professionals, unaffiliated with plan sponsors, to offer employees one-on-one, unbiased advice on their 401(k) investment choices.

Why should plan providers care? Because they know if you've built a relationship with someone else who has proven trustworthy, the likelihood of you choosing them to help you after you retire is about zero.

So there you have it. Hidden in plain sight. You are a commodity to large plan providers.

What can you do with this information? Educate yourself. Not with anger or resentment; but, with some measure of happiness because now you know the truth.

And, isn't that what you want? The truth.

Granted, you have a life. For many of you taking the time to become an investment expert is not high on your list. That's ok. You don't have to. Help is available where it wasn't only seven to ten years ago.

I've been studying the writings of Marcus Aurelius, an ancient Emperor of Rome. I'll offer you one of his notes to himself which I've written down for myself. He said:

"Don't be ashamed to need help. Like a soldier storming a wall, you have a mission to accomplish. And if you've been wounded and you need a comrade to pull you up? so what?"

Chapter Five
Understanding Your Role

In this section, let me take you through what it was like, what happened and what it's like now. Today, your successful retirement outcome depends on the role you choose to play. The key points covered here will help you play to win.

xoxoxo

How You Ended Up With a 401(k) Plan

There is something to be said for history. It helps put things in perspective. So the first step in understanding your role in this Employee "benefit" is to gain a perspective on what came before: the Pension Plan.

What ever happened to the pension plan, the retirement benefit that my father and your father probably had? You know, you work for a company for 30 years, get the gold watch and start collecting a monthly pension until the day you die. Usually like 80% of the salary you were making by the time you retired. What happened to that? Why do we have a 401(k) now, where you are responsible to put your money in and are responsible for being your own investment expert?

Basically what happened was, in your father's day, companies contributed some amount of profits every year to a retirement pool to be paid out to employees when they retired. It was called a defined benefit plan, because the benefit was known, well at least the formula was know. The key elements usually being years of service and something like the average of your last 5 years salary. The idea being that once you retired you would end up with about 80% of your salary to be paid out over your lifetime. It was a pretty common benefit to attract good talent.

What you had was the smartest guys in the room, members of an executive committee, maybe a few outside members of the Board of Directors, smart, well educated, A-type personalities, experienced in management, who knew how to delegate and were results driven. They were the most qualified guys to get the job done. They were responsible for overseeing this pool of money.

In the process, because they were smart enough to know what they didn't know, they hired the best investment professionals to invest the money for the benefit of the employees; and, they hired record keepers to keep track of how much money would be owed to individual employees and former employees already drawing benefits out of the pension plan; and, they hired CPAs to keep an eye on all of it.

Now the CPAs started looking at the amount of money in these pools. In fact they had been looking into the issue of accounting for the cost of pension plans since the mid-to-early 1950s. Primarily because the moral and legal obligation to pay current and future retirees did not appear in the audited financial statements - anywhere.

In this regard, the CPAs' mission was to provide the users of financial reports consistent information. It was believed that this Pension Plan Liability, because of the significance of the liability, would be important to determine the effect on the company's financial position and results of operations.

The point being, pension benefits were a cost of doing business, a labor cost, which was not being reflected on the books and records of the company. For users of financial statements this information would be useful not only to judge the company on its own; but, to compare it to its competitors.

So the CPAs pressed for the disclosure of the liability at least in the notes to the financial statements. Up until that point, none of this information was previously required. This was all "off balance sheet" stuff at the time. If I remember correctly, that was around the end of 1985 - Look up www.fasb.org Statement no. 87. "FASB" is short for the Financial Accounting Standards Board.

But what was the right number? What was the cost to the company for this off balance sheet, labor cost? So they brought in other experts called actuaries. They all sharpened their pencils. They made assumptions, such as the expected return on plan assets as well as the expected lives of retirees and other assumptions. They then calculated a present value of the expected future benefits the company was obligated to pay.

If the net present value number was greater than what was actually in the plan, they had a new number to disclose: the "unfunded liability."

Remember the idea was to come up with the projected benefit obligation so it could be compared to the actual money in the retirement plan.

Now when financial statements began to come out with the new employee pension cost numbers the investing public panicked when these unfunded liability numbers came to light. Remember, up until that point, no one was focusing on this because it was never required in the statements. Again, this was all off balance sheet stuff. Other than a line item expense about that year's contribution to the pension plan, the total amount of future benefits the company had promised to pay was not reported.

Suddenly, large public companies, literally overnight, were showing multi-million dollar liabilities for the cost of these employee pension plans they had not yet funded.

In turn, stock prices began to fall because the numbers were so massive that no one believed the companies would ever be able to match the unfunded portion without contributing unheard of amounts of company profits going forward. Profit that shareholders wanted for dividends, capital for reinvestment in the business and, in turn, future stock price increases.

Now, I'm sure pressure was brought to bear on the companies to do something; and, I am sure, the investment committee members, particularly the ones who were also employees themselves, became fearful for their jobs. And so the smartest guys in the room realized, we don't have to offer these plans. We are not required to offer this benefit. So, at the end of the day, they simply decided to terminate the pension plan.

They just stopped offering it to employees.

But now they had a recruitment problem. Because now they didn't have a retirement benefit to offer current and future employees. If they were looking to hire talent, and their competitors were offering some kind of retirement benefit and they were not, they were losing the chance to hire good employees. And, to a certain extent, they were also losing existing employees to the competition.

That's where the 401(k) came in. It was something. Not nearly as good as the Pension Plan was for employees. But it was something.

So, about 25 years ago the goal of the 401(k) was to make sure companies offering this new retirement plan would never again be liable for the benefits to be paid to retirees.

So the first part was to change who would pay for this benefit. No longer would it be just the company providing monies to employees out of profits.

The primary amount of money going into these plans was to come from employees out of their pay. The incentive to get employees to buy into this idea was the money to come out of your paycheck would be before taxes were applied.

The other characteristic of the 401(k) plan was that employees themselves would be responsible for investing these monies for their own future benefit; so again the company would avoid any legal liability for future benefits.

Finally, in order to make sure that companies would not be liable, companies were forbidden to give investment advice to the employee. So if you've ever gone to human resources and asked them to show you what you should invest in... Human resources would politely look at you and tell you they can't help you.

In fact, HR has been instructed they are not to help you with investment choices or even to suggest what they personally think might be the best investment option in the plan. Remember, companies are trying to avoid even the perception they are giving advice, which, in turn, may make them liable for investment outcomes.

So, we've basically gone from the smartest guys in the room with the assistance of professional experts to do the investment selection and the record-keeping along with CPAs to audit the numbers. We've moved to the point where the least financially sophisticated individual, the employee, is responsible for all of it on their own.

To put this in perspective for you, as of the first quarter of 2012, the total amount of money in US 401(k) plans was estimated at 3.4 trillion dollars.

Let's be honest here, if your education and experience is in engineering or sales or management or sigma six or human resources or customer service or social work or education or construction or marketing, what makes you an expert in investments?

Remember this is your retirement we're talking about here, and the line has been drawn in the sand, the only one responsible for it is you.

So what's the point? Why bother with this discussion? It's not to judge whether the 401(k) is right or wrong or good or bad or to blame anyone for where we are. The point is to let you know how we got here and the truth around any company's attitude around your retirement. Regardless of what they may say and how sincere they are about your future welfare. Their actions can only lead to one truth: you and you alone are responsible for your retirement.

It is what it is. And, being aware of the truth, you now have choices. I remember hearing long ago that the first step to escaping a prison is becoming aware that you are in prison.

What companies have not said and what Wall Street would rather you not know is: there is nothing to prevent you from getting whatever help you need from any source you choose, to guide you to your retirement goals. That help may be education so you can do it yourself or it may be guidance or advice from an expert to do it for you or something in between. Again, you're responsible.

I'll leave you with this thought, what I have learned over the past 30 years, the investment arena has many ways to extract money from you if you are not very educated about the process.

The market does not care if you win or lose. It does not care about genuine desires or good intentions. The investment markets, for as long as there have been investment markets, have changed and will continue to change. If you are unable or unwilling to adapt and change; if you are thinking that investing for your retirement is an event, picking something from your 401(k) plan and forgetting about it for twenty or thirty years; the market will be very happy to take your money.

xoxoxo

Are You Getting Advice

Let me start by telling you a short story. When I started out as an investment banker, working in the corporate finance department of a regional investment banking firm in December 1981, I had not been there five years when the head of the department was named chief executive officer of the firm. In the process, there was a write up published on his career at the firm; and, it said his first job at the firm was a customer's man.

I spoke to him sometime later and I asked him what is a customer's man? He told me it was a revered position in the firm with the nostalgia that only a man with white hair can possess.

The public title was "stockbroker" but inside the firm the title was "customer's man." I asked him why a stockbroker would be a revered position; and, he said a Customer's Man was the last line of defense between the customer and the products the firm was pushing at the customer.

The customer's man only ever had the best interest of the client at heart. He was honored to have been given this job. He was clearly proud.

What became of the Customer's Man? Hard to say; but, the loss has certainly been tough on customers. Today we have to choose between a "Stockbroker," "Financial Advisor," "Wealth Advisor," "Investment Strategist," "Registered Representative," "Vice President," and even "Managing Director." I've always thought Customer's Man was a remarkable title. Over the years I've been in the business I've seen a dwindling number of real customer's men.

And for the last 25 years, I have never seen a customer's man in the 401(k) space.

There are none. There is no last line of defense.

Despite whatever tools your employer may provide in your plan, informational brochures on how the plan works, how you opt-in, what investments are available, they can never give you advice. You may have free access to retirement calculators which will generate the familiar pie-chart. You may get free educational seminars to guide you through the process. You may get a call center employee at the financial company which your company selected to run the 401(k) plan to walk you through the process.

But you will never get specific investment advice. Period.

What is advice? Advice is an ongoing process. It is not an event. The reason your employer offers a 401(k) plan vs.. a pension plan is because the idea was to shift the burden of saving and investing for retirement directly to you, the employee.

Advice is making specific recommendations as to what products to use and exactly how much money to put into each product. It is a second set of eyes to let you know what to do when things go right; and, more importantly, what to do when things go wrong. Remember, the real trick to successful investing is to avoid catastrophic losses.

Advice is helping you construct a portfolio designed for you, personally. It includes the mutual understanding that as things change in your life, as well as in the investment markets, adjustments must be made.

Not so very long ago, Hurricane Sandy came roaring through the East Coast of the United States. Very few people ignored the advice to take shelter and adjust their lives. Where were the warnings in the financial markets during 2008? Did your company advise you to take shelter?

The simple truth is your employer cannot give you advice, free or otherwise.

Listen, if you think this doesn't matter because you are a "buy and hold investor" you had better sharpen your pencil because Buy and Hold only works in a bull market. We haven't been in a bull market for the past 12 years and there is no telling how much longer this cyclical bear market will last.

One last point, the financial industry, particularly in the mutual fund space, has spent millions upon millions of dollars spreading this advertising message. And, in truth, that is all it is, an ongoing advertising campaign.

How can you tell? Look at what they do vs.. what they say.

Go to the Morningstar website: www.morningstar.com.

Let's look at Fidelity Contrafund. This fund's ticker is FCNTX. Enter the ticker (FCNTX) into the "Quote" box. Find the headers just to the right of the dollar quote and the NAV day change beginning with Yield. To the right you will see Load, Total Assets, Expenses, Fee Level and Turnover. Turnover is the number we want to look at. In this example, the turnover rate is 55%.

What is turnover? It is a measure of the purchase and sale of stocks in a fund's portfolio over a twelve month period. So, a turnover of 100% would mean that the entire portfolio was sold and positions replaced over the last year. In the case of Fidelity Contrafund, over half the portfolio was replaced. Not exactly "buy and hold." Look up any actively managed mutual fund in your 401(k) line-up and I doubt you will see one with a turnover of 0%.

If you care to research the subject, you will discover any number of experts touting one side of the debate or the other. As for me the actions of the portfolio managers speak volumes. What it tells me is that "Stay the Course,"

"Stock for the Long Run," "It's Not Timing the Market but Time in the Market That Matters" are but clever and brilliant marketing slogans. The message to the individual investor is simply that this is too complicated and you would be foolish to try it on your own. Buy and hold is for you and not for us.

Don't forget, for the financial industry as a whole, this is a billion dollar business. They have a vested interest in keeping your assets under their roof. Yet, you only need look to the explosive growth of the Exchange Traded Fund segment of the market to realize that consumer awareness is on the rise.

The mutual fund industry is clinging to one of the last bastions left, the 401(k) plan. While many 401(k) plans are instituting a self directed brokerage option for their plan participants in compliance with the Pension Protection Act of 2006, there are those still holding out or limiting the investment options via this channel.

So, please be aware you are not getting advice.

xoxoxo

Common Obstacles You can Overcome…

A few days ago, a friend introduced me to a speaker whose two appearances on TED Talks have gone viral with almost 15 million views! She was new to me; but, I liked her immediately. She just strikes me as being very real. I think she would rather I call her a "Magic Pixie" than a story-teller but whatever you care to call her, I would highly recommend you watch her presentations. Her name is Brené Brown.

She's a research professor at the University of Houston, Graduate College of Social Work. She has spent the past ten years studying vulnerability, courage, authenticity, and shame. She spent the first five years of her decade-long study focusing on shame and empathy, and is now using that work to explore a concept that she calls Wholeheartedness. She poses the questions:

How do we learn to embrace our vulnerabilities and imperfections so that we can engage in our lives from a place of authenticity and worthiness? How do we cultivate the courage, compassion, and connection that we need to recognize that we are enough, that we are worthy of love, belonging, and joy?

At this point, you may be shaking your head wondering what the heck does this have to do with my 401(k)?

In my opinion, her work really does help connect the pieces, getting to the very root of why you may be having trouble with your retirement account.

The presentation my friend sent me was the one she did in March of 2012 titled "Listening to Shame." Near the end of her talk she mentioned the power of seduction. The seduction which tells us: I will enter the arena and kick some ass... once I'm bulletproof and I'm perfect. She said yes, that's seductive. But, the truth is that never happens.

That's the message shame serves up, particularly, in my opinion, when it comes to money and managing money, inside and outside your retirement account. Shame tells us we're not good enough; and, even if we can drive that message out, it comes back with "who do you think you are?" In turn, you may get seduced into thinking I'll just wait. I'll wait until I understand this perfectly so I don't screw it up because, after all, this is serious money.

And waiting turns into more waiting which fuels shame because we're unwilling or unable to make a decision. We're unsure. We have doubts. And then the message that we're not good enough plays over and over, every time the random thought of aging comes to mind or we hear a financial news report. Here's the point. It's a trap.

I've been in the industry over thirty years and I can tell you, you are not alone! No one, including myself, gets this perfect. Every professional in this industry makes mistakes. If you meet one who says he or she hasn't, slowly back away, because they are either lying or are in deep, deep denial.

Brené's research suggests if you want to grow shame in a petrie dish, shame on steroids, you only need three things: secrets, silence and judgement. (Self-judgement actually) Isn't this how today's retirement plans are structured? Outside the one hour or so 401(k) meeting your company put together for you, how many of you openly discuss your retirement account or money in general?

Your employer is forbidden to talk to you about what may be suitable choices for you. And, if you talk to those above you in your organization, you may feel weak or stupid or vulnerable. That's how shame feels. So the elements of secret keeping and silence are reinforced. Add to all that the self judgement: not good enough all over again... I don't know anything about investing or the stock market so how am I supposed to choose? Shame has everything it needs to flourish in this environment.

There are those too who have had the courage to seek outside help only to realize too late the advice they were given was not entirely in their best interest, Some of you have told me you had an advisor who was recommending choices motivated by their own, personal financial interest.

Again, we've all been there, not just in financial matters; but, that's how we learn. We make mistakes, we adjust, we move on. However it's one thing to trust a bad mechanic who fixes something needlessly which doesn't solve the problem you came in with or a bad plumber or housepainter or fix-it man; and, it is another to trust someone who stood by and watched while half your money went up in smoke.

This is the primary reason I started podcasting. Can I do this for you? Sure I can. It's what I do. But my goal here is to help you help yourself. You can do this. It's not brain surgery. The most basic, simple principals I have set out for you can be followed by anyone with just a little concentration. If nothing else, you can relieve yourself of the emotion and panic so common in the media because you will be able to see clearly what's happening with your choices.

Finally, Brené's research suggests the antidote to shame is empathy, finding others who say "really, me too!" So look around. How many people are in your company? How many of your friends and family work for companies where they have a 401(k) plan? How many people across the country work for companies which offer a 401(k) Plan? Believe me. You are not alone.

xoxoxo

Pandering to Safety...

Let's look at the relevance of risk, specifically risk avoidance, in light of the rising trend in life expectancy.

Why is this relevant? Let's look to a professor and chairman of the economics department at Harvard University, Greg Mankiw, who observed the number of years actually spent in retirement, comparing periods ending in 1970 vs. 2007. Yes. This study is already over 5 years old and I can only imagine people are living longer still.

In the US, a 66 year old male entering retirement in 1970 would've had to finance about nine years of retirement. A new retiree in 2007 would've had to finance twice as many years: about eighteen. And, recent studies I've seen, put the number well over twenty years. The point being, Who today can afford to rely on so called safe investments before and even after age 65? Outliving your money is a real issue.

Now, let's dovetail this with the default mode of human emotions: safety and risk avoidance. Some time ago I saw an article in the New York Times titled Anywhere the Eye Can See, It's Likely to See an Ad. And, one of the most widely recognized, effective elements of an Ad is what's called "Risk Reversal." You know it as - the ten day free trial or double your money back guarantee, as well as other ways to assure the consumer they are "safe." So the safety message is being seen by each of us thousands of times every day. No wonder we all crave safety!

Now this safety message is not exactly the same as the financial industry use of a "risk tolerance" questionnaire; but, this device does punch the same emotional triggers. It's asking the 401(k) investor to self-identify their tolerance for risk defined as short term, unrealized losses.

Even if you've opted out of managing your own investments by placing blind trust in a Target Date Fund you're still exposed to this hazard because by design Target Date Funds automatically take you out of historically higher return markets and push you into historically lower return markets. So when you reach your target retirement age you have an overwhelming proportion of your portfolio in so called "safe" assets. By design, Target Date Fund Managers are pandering to your emotional craving for "safe" assets.

Let me play devil's advocate for a moment. Suppose I told you there *are no* "safe" investments. The naked truth is, all investing is a trade-off. Want low volatility? You can achieve it by buying bonds (vs. Bond Funds) but the trade off is accepting the possible loss of purchasing power. You may be taking on *inflation* risk in exchange for the *idea* your money is safe in bonds (which it is not, by the way because, regardless of the credit rating, there is always the *possibility* of a default and you won't get your money back)

Isn't this what happened during the financial crisis in 2008? The industry manufactured a AAA rated asset class out of risky mortgages, regulators mostly applauded at the time, and the regulations explicitly told banks AAA paper was safe. The banks told you and everyone was happy, right up to the point they were not, when these assets were quite suddenly deemed unsafe.

Why? Because the the device to make them seem safe failed. The device was a guarantee from a financial institution which promised to cover any defaults on the mortgages. It was a guarantee and promise for which they charged a fee. They never imagined the overwhelming number of defaults which took place. In turn, they defaulted on their promise.

Lets stop for a moment and look at The Library of Economics and Liberty website. Particularly at a post by Arnold Kling who received his Ph.D. in economics from MIT in 1980 and served as an economist on the staff of the Board of Governors of the Federal Reserve System from 1980-1986. His post titled Remarks on Safe Assets suggests... and I quote: "Because very few people really understand risk, there tends to be a lot of potential profit to be made by taking *advantage* of people's *desire* for assets that *appear* safe, even if they are not."

What happens to your chances of living out *all* your retirement years filled with freedom, pleasure, dignity and financial independence if you trade the *illusion* of safety for a return on assets you could have had?

What will be the average life expectancy in retirement when you reach age 65? Twenty-five years? Thirty years? More? If you continue doing what you have been doing so far, will it be enough of a nest egg to see you all the way through?

Just remember, Target Date Funds are not a guarantee and neither is the asset allocation strategy most 401(k) plans promote. We live in a world where you are responsible for your own retirement funding.

Ignoring that fact won't change it anymore than ignoring gravity will prevent you from falling. Putting blind faith in a Target Date Fund won't change it. And, Turning it all over to a financial advisor won't change it either.

You must have some level of involvement if only to keep an eye on the ball.

The solution for you then is to detach from the notion that you "need" safety particularly when "risk" is defined as fluctuating portfolio values. The time you need to be most concerned with portfolio values is when you have to withdrawal money from the account. Remember that investment markets are dynamic. Prices will fluctuate. It is normal.

My commitment to you is to show you a logical, organized, systematic way to measure the investments in your plan. Once you understand the method, you will no longer view "safety" in terms of market volatility. You will understand "safety" for what it is: true preservation of capital and managing your downside risk of capital loss. In the process, global events and concern over government policy will not leave you unsure about your portfolio.

xoxoxo

Why Your Role is Critical

Hopefully by this point in your reading, you are beginning to understand you need to play a role in this process. Buy and Hold and Set-it-and-forget-it may not get you the retirement outcome you deserve.

So let's focus on probably the most important principal of wealth accumulation: avoiding catastrophic losses. Sophisticated investors have known this for thousands of years. It's very difficult to build real wealth if you do not even try to manage the downside risk because trying to recover from those losses may tempt you to take bigger and bigger bets.

When I was a young man, I used to play, once a week, late night cards with a half dozen friends. Definitely not high-stakes, just dime, nickel quarter type of bets. The "big" winner for an evening might walk away with fifty dollars. To keep it friendly, the house rule was the winner for the evening would have to treat everyone else to breakfast out.

I remember one game there was a new guy playing and lady luck was not smiling on him. The thing was, of all of us, he really couldn't afford to be losing. But, he kept betting, even when he knew and everyone at the table knew, he just didn't have the cards. When I asked him what the heck he was doing he just said "I have to" and while we all felt sorry for him we weren't particularly charitable. I think he ended the evening losing about seventy-five dollars.

The point is he kept chasing his money. Well, what he thought was his money, despite the fact he'd already lost it. In the process, he kept taking risks which were just silly.

So let's bring this to your 401(k). What kind of gain would you need to make up for losses in your account? Here is the math. Say a $100,000 account loses $20,000 which is a 20% loss. In order to get back to $100,000 you will need a gain of 25%. To recover from a $30,000 loss (30%) you will need a 43% gain; a $40,000 loss (40%) will require a 67% gain; and, a $50,000 loss (50%) will require a 100% gain.
Can you see how these losses and the required gains *just to break even* are staggering?

One of the things I do to monitor the pulse of the 401(k) industry is simple keyword research. I am surprised at the number of people out there who are cheering because recent market returns have increased their accounts. There seems to be a collective denial about what's happened since 2007.

I've seen accounts where the dollar value is about where it was in 2007 and the owner seems happy; but, the joy is lost when they count all the new money (their contribution plus any company match) that has been added to the account over the last 5 years or 60 months. And, their thinking was, before we both analyzed the account, that they finally broke even.

Can you imagine how your account would look if you had avoided most of the losses in 2008 even if you had missed some of the gains in 2009?

Let's run a quick hypothetical to make the point. Let's assume you had a million dollars in your account on September 28, 2007 invested in an S&P index. By September 30, 2008 you had lost $230,000 - 23% and decided to sell out. You waited until July 31, 2009 before you repurchased the S&P index with your remaining $770,000 and did nothing else thru Jan. 31, 2013. You would have $1,170,400. Had you just held on from September 28, 2007 you would have $981,240. You would have earned $189,000 for having managed the downside risk.

Again this is a hypothetical. It assumes no new money, no dividends or interest and the exit and reentry into the market were chosen simply to make a point.

Avoiding catastrophic losses is part of the investment process. My dad, in his youth, was a volunteer fireman - they called them firehose drills. It was learning what to do before they were called to a burning building.

Remember, whatever mutual fund you may own in your 401(k) they are not going to manage the downside risk for you. Managing the downside risk is your job. And, if you are thinking about hiding out in a bond fund in your 401(k), you may want to consider the 30 year bull market in bonds, according to noted experts in the field, is over. Bond funds may not be all that safe anymore.

xoxoxo

Focus on What's Important

Imagine you are walking down the street thinking about your plans for the day.

Suddenly, someone walking toward you "accidentally" drops a grocery bag. And, while you are kindly bending over to help with the spilled articles, another member of the team lifts your wallet. The first person thanks you profusely for your help; you say "it was no trouble" and go happily on your way… only to discover hours later your wallet is missing.

According to Wikipedia, pickpocketing is a form of larceny that involves the stealing of money or other valuables from the pocket or purse of a victim without their noticing the theft at the time. It requires considerable dexterity and a knack for misdirection.

For months now there has been a battle going on in the 401(k) space around the new requirement to shine a light on the fees employees have been paying for their 401(k) investments.

Why this new disclosure requirement? Well, there was a survey done not too long ago where about 70% of employees said they didn't know they were paying anything for their 401(k).

Why? Well, because it's been the industry practice all along for mutual fund companies to simply deduct their fees directly out of a customer's account, without sending them an invoice or notice each time fees are deducted.

This practice is nothing new and the process is clearly described in the Prospectus you get when you choose an investment in your 401(k) plan. Yet, most people miss it or forget it very quickly.

What I find fascinating about all this is the marketing spin. So far, the media has been directing attention around the injustice of the industry practice with the same indignation one may feel after discovering they've been a mark for a pickpocket. One moment you have your wallet and your money and the next moment it's gone.

The media drama has been around the years of "lost" savings over a working career because of these fees.

I have seen article after article, spinning and re-spinning this message; and, even some suggesting how to pressure your company into changing the investment line-up to get more "low-cost" 401(k) options into the plan while dumping high-fee options.

Now, the question I ask myself is… Is it possible this focus has been orchestrated?

Is this just another form of misdirection and dexterity to pick your pocket? Is it possible the intent is to keep the focus off what may really help you?

If the thought has crossed your mind to force your company to adopt lower fee investment options, you may want to stop for just a moment and ask yourself, what am I missing?

You see, I believe this discussion deliberately misses the point. If you are like the 70% of employees who didn't know you were paying fees from your own account; and, you're upset, that's a good thing. The question is what to do about it.

Ask yourself, how will you be served spending energy to simply change the investment line-up?

Did you know there is already a process in place to help you control expenses in your account? This process is spelled out in The Pension Protection Act of 2006 which came into effect in January 2008.

There are two relevant provisions in the Act, both of which direct 401(k) plan providers to do something they have absolutely no financial incentive to do. The first part is offering your company the option of offering you, the employee, a self-directed brokerage account within your plan.

The second part is offering your company the option of offering you, the employee, with a process to use your own 401(k) money, on a pre-tax basis, to hire an investment advisor of your choosing, who is in no way affiliated with or beholding to the provider of your plan.

Think about why 401(k) Plan Providers want to keep the focus away from these choices? Don't forget how BIG this is. In the US alone, it's been reported there are 3.4 Trillion Dollars in 401(k) accounts at the end of the 1st quarter of 2012. That's 3,400,000,000,000 (that's eleven zeros people!). When you get a chance, grab a pen and write 3-4 followed by eleven zeros. It's mind boggling.

If you assume the average 401(k) investor pays about 8/10 ths of one percent of their account balance annually in fees, this translates into annual fees of 27.2 BILLION dollars!

I have to tell on myself, because I had to calculate this number three different ways. I don't know why, but the number surprised me. It just didn't seem believable.

Think about it, do you believe an industry making *annual* fees of 27.2 BILLION dollars isn't going to go to any length to protect their own financial interest?

So, what happens to these fees if your company adopts a self-directed brokerage account option for employees? Well, if it's done in keeping with the *spirit* of The Pension Protection Act of 2006, meaning the account established is no more restrictive than an IRA (an individual retirement account) the plan provider will lose much of the fees from assets transferred into these accounts because the plan provider will only be providing a brokerage function.

Sure, they will get a small commission on handling the transaction; but, no *annual* fees. If you choose to buy a mutual fund or even an exchange traded fund inside the self-directed brokerage account, yes, there will be annual fees; *but*, you can easily control those fees by selecting the best performing, lowest cost funds available in the entire market not just the 12 or so funds offered in the typical plan. Or, you can invest in individual stocks and bonds, in which case, you will not pay annual fees.

Also, why would 401(k) Plan Providers not want you, the employee, to have a process to use your own 401(k) money, on a pre-tax basis, to hire an investment advisor who is in no way affiliated with or beholding to the provider of your plan?

The end-goal for the Plan Provider is to have the first chance to convince you to roll over your 401(k) when you retire into their company's IRA account. Ever wonder why you never personally hear from your Plan Provider until you are close to retirement and then they start phone calls, direct mail and e-mail to get you to roll-over your 401(k)? Because capturing your retirement assets in a Rollover IRA is the cherry on top of the 401(k) plan business.

If you have been successfully advised for years by an advisor, with *integrity*, not affiliated with the Plan Provider, and with whom you have developed a *relationship*, how likely is it the Plan Provider will be able to capture your assets when you leave the company?

The answer is not very. So Plan Provider will try very hard to keep these advisors away from you. They are real competition for your assets especially when you consider your plan provider does nothing to develop a personal *relationship* with you.

So, if you are going to spend one moment trying to effect a change at your company, why not spend that energy pushing for a change that will really matter to you. Petition your company to adopt a self directed brokerage account option and the option to pay for a financial advisor of your own choosing directly out of your own account using pre-tax dollars?

The point of The Pension Protection Act of 2006 was to level the playing field for employees to get unbiased advice. The point of the new fee disclosure rules was to first help employees become aware that they are and have been paying fees all along and to let employees know they have choices.

In my opinion, the media drama around the fees you have been paying is simply another form of clever misdirection to distract you from what is in your best interest: the chance to develop a relationship with a professional of your own choosing, with integrity, who is beholding to no one but you, who is willing to be the last line of defense between you and the financial products being pushed at you.

xoxoxo

The #1 Investor Challenge of Today

Information overload. While the information age has been a boon for all of us, it has a downside: information overload.

If everything is important then nothing is more important than anything else.

It makes it impossible to make sense of anything because the default mode of thinking in the face of overwhelming information is to ignore all of it!

In this wonderful modern age we live in, everyone is busy... and distracted. So it is no wonder most people find their retirement benefits more confusing than their health care benefits. The primary reason is the overwhelming amount of information employees are expected to consume without any meaningful way to filter it to make better choices.

One of the things I have done for myself which I find helpful, is to set up alerts on Google for 401(k) topics. It's a real timesaver because it frees me from running searches or just surfing around the internet hoping to find news and developments in the 401(k) industry.

If you have a google account, just go to google.com/alerts and you can set your own key word or phrase. Google will monitor the web and will deliver links to your email whenever new content is posted on the web. Check it out.

I no longer need to depend on the mainstream financial media scanning countless headlines promoting "breaking news" stories which never provide actionable information.

Some of the headlines crossing the tape recently:

1. Why the US tax Bonanza maybe tapped out,
2. Has Apple lost it's genius?
3. Bank of America agrees to $10 billion dollar settlement for mortgage claims,
4. Stocks lower; S&P eases from five year high,
5. Is your credit score hurting your love life?

Come on is any of that relevant or actionable?!

I am going to repeat myself because this is really important for you: If everything is important then nothing is more important than anything else. It makes it impossible to make sense of anything because the default mode of thinking in the face of overwhelming information is to ignore all of it.

The consequence of this default mode of thinking is it creates a defeatist, victim mentality.

1. My 401(k) sucks,
2. The market is Rigged,
3. Wall Street is for suckers, and,
4. I'll never be able to retire.

The truth is all these statements are true if you allow yourself to drift along with whatever direction the market is moving: believing what Wall Street says versus what Wall Street does; and, believe that automatic enrollment in a target date fund will save you.

The benefit of setting up Google alerts for me is it gives me assurance that Google is delivering all the relevant information I need. Not because all of it is important; but, because it gives me a set of data to filter *for what is* important.

The goal of the 401(k) Owners Manual is to help you take the information overload around your 401(k) investment choices and filter it down to a simple, manageable relevant amount of information. The principles we discuss here focused on measuring what is… taking only the relevant information in the market and using that information to make better 401(k) investment decisions.

One of our Podcast listeners told me: "I'm loving watching all the political intrigue and just tracking the numbers. It really removes so much of the emotion and panic I see around me."

But, before we get to that, there are a few more things to bring to your attention.

xoxoxo

The Seven Deadly Investment Mind-Games

The information overload just discussed is one of the causes of the next topic: mindset. Specifically *negative* mindset which is common among even professional investors. Actually, I've list more than seven; but, the title is catchy!

The reason for going over these is... by recognizing these habits of thought you can then learn to change them. Make no mistake, I've been doing this for decades and I still catch myself falling into these patterns. I just recognize them quicker now, and in the process, I get to laugh at myself.

Let's start with "Overgeneralization." Basically this is the habit of coming to a general conclusion based on a single piece of evidence or event. If something bad happened once you expect it to happen over and over again. The tip-off is when words like "always" and "never" come to mind. For example: I lost money in the dot-com bubble. I'll never buy tech stocks again. Or, I lost half my 401(k) in 2008. I'll always be poor.

Next is "Filtering," which is ignoring important information that doesn't support your negative view of the situation. Does your thinking sound like this? The financial media is still talking about how bad the economy is so, it's a good thing I've kept my money in cash. The market gains over the last twenty months won't last anyway.

Then there's "All or Nothing" or black and white thinking. This is thinking in terms of extremes: failing to explore more modest solutions. I've already lost 30% in this investment so there's no point in selling now. Or. I'm up 50%. I'd better sell it all before I lose it.

Ever catch yourself "Personalizing"? Thinking what people say or do is somehow related to you or a reaction to you. Like: I couldn't get anyone on the phone to change my asset allocation yesterday and now the market is down 500 points. They must have caller ID over there! Or, how about: Those people in HR must not like me because they told me I couldn't use my 401(k) to invest in

80

my uncle's startup company.

"Catastrophizing"? Overestimating the chances of disaster. If I sell now, the market will go up 90%! Or, no, I always buy high and ride the price into the ground.

How about "Fortune Telling"? Assuming your prediction about an anticipated outcome is actually a fact. The markets are rigged so there's no point investing. Or, I've never made money in the market so why should I waste my time looking at investment options. The big problem with this mindset is it can actually become self-fulfilling.

"Should Statements" are a good one. Beating yourself up over unrealistic expectations of yourself or others. Sound familiar: I should have bought Microsoft when they went public or McDonalds or Apple. Or, I should never have bought my company's stock because the boss told me it was a good deal.

And, finally, "Emotional Reasoning" which is mistaking feelings for facts. I lost money in the market. I feel like a failure, therefore I am a failure.

Which can lead to "Mind Reading" which is assuming you *know* what other people will think and say and do without actually checking in with them. Like, my spouse will be furious because the 401(k) lost money so I have to hide the account statement. Or, If I win big in the market everyone will be happy.

So here are some tips for getting your Mindset straight which may help with investing and life in general.

The first step is to Listen to yourself. I've never done it but some have actually taken a notepad and written out the negative thoughts which have crossed their mind during the course of a day. Seeing it on paper can be just the shock to get you motivated to take the next step.

Next is being as honest as you can with yourself. If your brain goes to one of the negative Mindsets about money, here is a great tip. Ask yourself, literally, Is this true? Is it logical? Take the example of "I lost money in the dot-com bubble. I'll never buy tech stocks again" The truth is it's not logical, it's emotional. You may have lost money; but, that's not to say you will ALWAYS lose money.

If those questions are difficult to answer: Try this one: Can you *absolutely* know it's true?

Throughout my career, I've heard it said individual investors are ruled by fear and greed. The common thread in all the Negative Mindset patterns we just covered is fear.

To this day, I get a knot in my stomach when someone recommends a retail stock. There is no rule which says you should never invest in retail industry stocks.

My personal track record investing in retail stocks hasn't been particularly bad; I just feel like it's a seasonal bet and I'm not willing to hold them long term. That's just me.

I'm aware of it and rather than getting all stressed out over it. I just take as much of the emotion out of it as I'm able. For me the tool I turn to is the Point & Figure chart because it measures what is; and, that's usually enough to take most of the emotion out of the decision. I'll tell you more about Point & Figure charts later in the book.

Two other habits I've taught myself is to first avoid the comparison game; and, second is to look at the big picture. In Investing, it's very tempting to play the "Should" game. I should have bought this rather than what I did buy. This is just a form of magical thinking designed to beat myself up. It is a cleverly disguised regret.

The way to challenge this kind of Mindset is to simply ask "Would I buy that 'other' investment today"? If the answer is no, that's the end of the mental discussion. If the answer is yes, then I have some decisions to make.

Looking at the Big Picture is a great exercise because it puts things in their true perspective. If I am grappling with what to do about an investment loss, if I can put it in perspective relative to my entire net worth that usually takes the stress out of any decision. So, any decision can be calmed by honestly asking the question: How important is it, really? Or, Is this really a big deal?

In short, what I've found most effective is to either counter or replace these negative mindsets with realistic, positive ones. Don't ever try to suppress a negative thought. It doesn't work. You need to substitute another in it's place. Actually change your mind. It can be done! By the way, these tools help with just about any area of your life not just investing.

xoxoxo

Master or Slave

What a remarkable life. I recently discovered the writings of a man who lived over one thousand, eight hundred years ago. An Emperor of Rome by the name of Marcus Aurelius, who lived in the years 121 to 180 after the death of Christ. It's assumed these writings, titled simply, Meditations, were written later in his life and were never intended for publication.

It seems the subject of his personal writing to himself, alone, centered on his spiritual and ethical beliefs. His writings contain practical advise on everything from living in the world to coping with adversity. He had a profound understanding of human behavior. I've already found more wisdom in it than I can absorb in a single reading. Grab yourself a copy. You won't regret it.

Today I wanted to focus on one short reminder he wrote to himself which goes like this:

"Love the discipline you know, and let it support you. Entrust everything willingly to the gods, and then make your way through life, no one's master and no one's slave."

Thinking about your 401(k) and what it represents, I cannot help but wonder about the impact of a trend which seems to be emerging. Fidelity Investments began tracking "cash-out" data in 2009. The activity being measured here is the number of employees who have cashed-out their 401(k) retirement savings particularly when leaving one employer for another and using the money for non-retirement spending.

To put this in perspective, Federal Reserve data suggests $36 billion was cashed-out in 2004 while $60 billion was drained in 2010. According to Fidelity, of the plans it manages, 35 percent of all participants cashed out their 401(k) balances when leaving their jobs last year, and the trend was even worse for young and lower income workers.

Taking this back to the Emperor's advice to himself, are we seeing a population, here in the United States, consciously or unconsciously leading themselves into slavery?

Again. Perspective. What is a slave? One definition is: a person who is excessively dependent upon or controlled by someone or something. The other day, Forbes Magazine presented an article in which the author stated:

The reason most of us save is so that we can afford to maintain our living standard after we retire. This requires we be able to afford the goods and services that we rely upon, and to do so whether we live to 80, 90, 100 years old or beyond.

What becomes of this ability if savings are cashed out for non-retirement spending? The obvious answer is we lose self-control. We become slaves. Will we become excessively dependent upon friends, family, or governments?

Is the 401(k) plan structure perfect? No. I don't believe it is. I've pointed out any number of flaws and many of them you alone, are powerless to change. However, it is what we have to work with. It is the discipline we know and I believe it can support you.

Not however, without your *real* participation. What that means is you have to actually put aside money from your income, take whatever match your company will provide; *and*, you have to invest and grow that money *and* protect it from catastrophic losses along the way.

Fortunately, all of this is possible with a small amount of personal effort. You don't need an MBA or even a college degree.

Now I've heard people say they're getting grey hair waiting for their 401(k) to work. They cry about how after the dot com bubble, the liquidity crisis in 2008 and the recession it's just not grown at all.

Yet, these same people have been relying on a misguided belief that they don't have to manage the investments themselves. They believe their Plan Provider is responsible to do that for them. Unfortunately, that's not the way these plans work. They were never designed to work that way.

Don't accept these tools because I say you should. Look them over. Reason them out with someone else. Determine for yourself if they will work for you.

xoxoxo

What Do People Really Want...

I saw a presentation given some time ago by Dr. Frank I. Luntz. From his Biography in his most recent book, he is described as "one of the most respected communications professionals in America today." He was there to present data from thousands of ongoing focus groups he conducts. One of the slides he displayed showed the overwhelming lack of trust people have in

Corporate America. 75% were unable to say they have a good or great deal of trust in Fortune 500 CEO's; and, 71% could not say the same for the corporations themselves. The slide was titled Nobody Trusts Corporations.

He went on to explain why. Because people are sick and tired of promises or even pledges which have not been kept. So much so, that when they hear the words, "promise" or "pledge" they don't even want to hear the message. Dovetail this with the following...

FACT: Fidelity just released a study based on an analysis of 13 million participants in Fidelity 401(k) plans across the country showing about two-thirds of workers are managing their own 401(k) investments; but, about half of them are not taking an active role in managing their accounts.

FACT: another study reported on bloomburg.com recently noted Affluent millennials hold fifty-two percent of their money in cash.

FACT: Drawing from the Bloomburg article: As the oldest millennials approached college graduation in 2002, they witnessed a 78 percent plunge in the Nasdaq index as the bubble in technology shares burst. As they reached their mid-twenties in 2008, the Standard & Poor's 500 Index dropped 38.5 percent, the worst single-year performance since 1937. The gauge dropped 57 percent from October 2007 through March 2009.

And:

FACT: An MFS Survey released in February noted about 46 percent of millennials with more than $100,000 to invest say they will never be comfortable in the stock market. MFS Investment Management is an American-based global asset manager, formerly known as Massachusetts Financial Services.

Obviously, The current system isn't working... If the millennial generation is refusing to invest money for their own future... something is broken.

In my opinion, The Buy and Hold / Modern Portfolio Theory promise of risk management is broken and trust has been lost.

One thing I have personally observed over the years is we care most about what we're involved in directly. It has been my personal commitment to help you get directly involved in your 401(k) by giving you the common sense tools you can use now to efficiently and effectively take control of your own retirement money without the fear of economic uncertainty.

I believe you've worked hard for your money and protecting it can be a calm and methodical process.

xoxoxo

Discovering Choices...

Anyone who knows me, knows I'm totally on your side. I want you to succeed. And it's so frustrating to me when I see FACTS just mentioned about the millennial generation.

Back in March of 2010, Greg Mankiw, a professor and chairman of the economics department at Harvard University, did a blog post with a graphic from The Economist magazine. The graph showed the average US 66-year old retiree spends another 15-20 years in retirement.

The data set was from 2002 - 2007. Whereas the 1965 to 1970 data set showed something like 9 years. I can only imagine that by the time millennials get to age 66 their life expectancy will be much, much longer.

I don't believe anyone would challenge the idea that investment performance is going to be even more important over a post retirement life expectancy of twenty plus years.

So I've been wondering, is there a flaw in the behavior of millennials we just discussed? Is their reluctance purely emotional?

So, before I started writing today, I used a trick I learned which I'll share with you. I go for a long walk. It's amazing what happens when you start to move the big muscles. The brain begins to clear.

What came to me was IF the study is accurate and millennials hold 52 percent of their wealth in cash... and IF the reasoning is because they witnessed a 78 percent plunge in the Nasdaq index as the oldest of them approached college graduation in 2002. And, as they reached their mid-twenties in 2008, the Standard & Poor's 500 Index dropped 38.5 percent, and they watched in disbelief as it fell 57 percent from October 2007 through March 2009.

The idea came to me that these reasons are not the reasons. They are the results. They are the results of buy and hold. They are the results of the promise made that just spreading your assets in a so-called appropriate manner would be

86

sufficient to protect you from market losses.

Now here's the thing. Markets are not markets unless there are buyers AND sellers. The FACT is... the Nasdaq fell 78% in 2002 because there were more sellers than buyers. The reason the Standard & Poor's 500 Index dropped 38.5% in 2008 was because, again, there were more sellers than buyers. The gauge dropped 57 percent from October 2007 through March 2009 because there were more sellers than buyers.

The 401(k) plan participants who experienced losses similar to these is because they believed the buy and hold story they were sold. If you remember only one thing, remember this... Not everyone experienced these losses! That is a FACT. Why? Because there had to be sellers to drive the prices to these levels. A market transaction cannot take place without a willing buyer AND a willing seller.

You did not have to experience these losses then and you do not have to experience them any time in the future IF... you are willing to be a seller... sometimes.

I am guessing, and I assure you this is just a guess, what millennials are signaling to Wall Street is they do not believe in buy and hold and they will park their money in cash until they are shown a better system.

Chapter Six
Forensic Discoveries

Forensic science requires the collection and analysis of evidence which is relevant. In this section, we'll give you twenty-three areas to ponder. Some of these you may already know. Others may be entirely new to you. The purpose is to present the ideas and allow you to make your own decision how they may be personally useful to break down barriers to making better decisions.

xoxoxo

There will Never be "More" Time

Obviously retirement saving and investing is a tomorrow issue. Some would say it is the ultimate tomorrow issue. And, because it is a tomorrow issue, any number of people feel it's not something they need to focus on now.

Someday I'll get to it; but, not now. I've got more important things to do now. I don't have time to learn how to be an investment expert and work my job and raise a family and do all the chores on my to-do list. I'll wait until I have more time. I'll worry about it tomorrow.

The flaw in this thinking however is it's squandering the one element of investing you can never reclaim: time. So, if you keep putting off saving or ignore your investments you are selling yourself short because you can never make up that time.

The fact is there will never be "more" time. You don't get a chance to do it over. Someday may become never or you will have so little time left, you cannot make enough of an impact to retire when you want. The phrase "It's never too late." Does not apply here.

But suppose I told you there was a pay-off now? Suppose there was an immediate benefit for saving and investing for your future? Something you could get now. Right now. Not decades from now; but, right now?

What if the choices you make now allow you to feel better about yourself…
more so than you've ever felt in your life? Suppose the pay-off was being able to
own the feeling that you are smart and you do deserve to be happy about your
today and your tomorrows? Suppose the benefit you could get now was self-
confidence and self-esteem? You can, you know.

But, what if you're not an investment expert today? How much time will it
take? What will it cost?

Well, what do you know about medicine? Do you have a medical degree? No?
Does that stop you from taking your temperature? Does that stop you from
doing what you can to care for your own health? Do you take care of yourself,
like the rest of us, until it gets to the point you cannot do it yourself and then go
to an expert?

Perhaps some ancient wisdom may be of help. Here's a quote I saw from the
book titled Meditations which consists of the writings of Marcus Aurelius,
Emperor of Rome, who lived from 121-180 AD. It impressed me when he was
describing all the character traits he admired about his adopted father, 15th
Emperor of the Roman Empire, Antoninus Pius.

He said, describing his adopted father: "This, in particular: his willingness to
yield the floor to experts, in oratory, law, psychology, whatever, and to support
them energetically, so that each of them could fulfill his potential." Pretty
impressive for a Roman Emperor.

I will repeat another quote of Marcus Aurelius:

"Don't be ashamed to need help. Like a soldier storming a wall, you have a
mission to accomplish. And if you've been wounded and you need a comrade
to pull you up? So what?"

Listen, all of us have a mission - to glide into retirement with enough financial
resources to enjoy a life of happiness and dignity. I know you know this.
Procrastination is a decision. Main stream financial media doesn't help.
Making lists doesn't help. Waiting on the next Publication of the Federal
Reserve doesn't help. Analyzing research reports and reading financial
newspapers doesn't help.

Why? Because stock market investing is not always about the "best" company
or "best" management or "best" product or the "best" economic news. It's
about tracking the price movement of a stock and following the trend. If you

break it down to the two activities you must do right more often than not. All you have to do is buy it right and sell it right.

Face it. You're not Warren Buffett. You're never going to buy enough stock to own a company the way he does. He doesn't care about the price of a stock. He cares about the free cash flow the company produces. He's buying businesses, not stocks. You don't have that luxury so all you can do is watch the price. Economics 101. Supply and demand.

Suppose you took control of tracking the price movement of your investments so you could tell if the spin Wall Street was dishing out was true or not. Suppose you could laugh at the financial news or perhaps ignore it altogether?

How good will it feel to stop looking at your 401(k) time after time and still not know what to do with it? How good will it feel to stop asking yourself: Do I deserve this? Does it feel fair? If the price changes, will I feel smart or dumb? What will my neighbors think? What will my spouse think?

What if you stop allowing others to make decisions for you and then criticize you for it?

Isn't this what's happened over the past decade? Wall Street put you into these so called managed products. Told you it was safe to set-it-and-forget-it. Then when they lost your money they told you it was your fault… you wouldn't reach your retirement goals because you weren't saving enough. Rather than admit their Modern Portfolio Theory may actually be wrong, it's simpler to blame you. You weren't giving them enough money to work with.

xoxoxo

Beware the Law of Averages

Today is April 4th, 2013. The 1st Quarter of the year has closed and the S&P 500 Index is hovering right around 1550, right up there near the highs of July 2007 and Jan 2000, significant because just beyond those two dates the Index fell to right around 800!

The financial media has been buzzing with what happens now. Will we see a repeat of the last two corrections which took your breath away? As for me, I have no idea. I'll just keep watching the data day by day and make decisions based on what is.

Which brings me to our topic. Over the years, one of the more curious things

I've seen is the investment industry and the public's fixation on averages, to the point we believe they have some real meaning.

I recall an investment advisor I know sitting down with a client for their first annual review of the client's account, I guess it was some time during the 1st Quarter of 2002 and he told me his client kept asking where was his 10% return? Apparently, that was what the client heard when the advisor was courting him for the account before the correction began. The client kept insisting, You said the average return in the stock market has historically been 10%. I want my 10%. Where is it?

Now I know this advisor and while I wasn't there during his first meeting with this client, I would bet he never guaranteed this fellow a 10% return; but, that's clearly what the client expected. It's what he wanted to believe. Clearly this meeting in 2002 didn't go well.

"Past performance is not indicative of future returns" but, for whatever reason people easily, naively, want to ignore the wide variations of the markets and the results can lead to disaster. Yet, Wall Street's mantra of "Buy and Hold" and dollar cost averaging really are suggesting that past performance IS indicative of future returns, that investors simply need to stay the course and all will be well.

Tell that to someone who retired on schedule in January 2008 thinking they could draw down $60,000 every January on an $800,000 retirement account. If they thought they would get an average 10% return year after year and would be able to grow the account because they weren't taking all the returns, they would be looking at an account value less than half of what they started with now five years into retirement. It's unlikely they will ever see the account return to the $800,000 mark, especially if they continue drawing down the $60,000.

So investors need to consider not only the likelihood they will not experience some average return year in and year out over their retirement years, they need to consider the consequences of being wrong. The most fearful consequence being you will outlive your money and will be too old or too weak to re-enter the workforce.

Oh, too, don't forget the same trap relying on averages applies to your life expectancy as well. If you are figuring your rate of withdrawals based on an average life expectancy, remember, by definition, half of all people will live past the average.

Getting back to Average Returns and to help with perspective, I remember a great article in the New York Times in Jan. 2011. The title was "In investing, it's when you start AND when you finish." The point of the article is that returns become relatively stable... once you consider 60 to 70 years of data. Clearly this time frame isn't relevant over a normal retirement. If you study the chart, it becomes very clear very fast that market returns over any 20 year period you care to look at, are far more volatile than most people realize.

And, if this New York Times graph isn't enough to open your eyes, don't forget inflation. Even modest amounts of inflation will require additional dollars just to maintain the kind of lifestyle you want in retirement. The longer you live, the more inflation will eat into the buying power of your retirement assets.

Remember, the job of the Federal Reserve Bank is not to stop inflation, it's to control the rate of growth of inflation. Our Fed has taken on the role of central planner to create inflation because it's good for the economy / banking industry.

Anyway, do some planning with financial calculators (you can find them easily on the internet) to see what you should be saving for retirement and how long those savings will last. Run a number of scenarios with dramatically different assumptions about investment return and inflation.

Also, revisit the planning process frequently. Don't treat it as a one time exercise.

If you believe, and I do, it is unlikely you will ever see an average year, then you need to put things in their true perspective. Once you retire, the accumulation phase of wealth building is mostly behind you. Time is no longer on your side.

xoxoxo

Expectations

I've heard it said that an expectation is a premeditated resentment. So it makes sense to examine your expectations, particularly where your retirement money is concerned.

For the last thirty plus years I've been involved in the investment industry. The one topic I've seen which is rarely addressed is expectations.

Other than hearing the platitude from senior investment executives "you need to manage your customer's expectations," I don't believe I've ever heard about someone sitting down with a client or a prospect where expectations was a line item on the agenda.

So let's put it out there. Expectations.

As an employee, you expect to be paid for your contribution to the company. If paychecks are late or haven't been delivered for a while, you'd become concerned. You'd likely start looking around for other employment.

Depending on the size of your employer you would expect them to offer other benefits for your service like health care and retirement. Since few employers offer a pension anymore, your retirement benefit is likely a defined contribution plan: a 401(k) or a 503b.

Wrapped around those retirement benefits are expectations. Particularly the expectation that the money you and your employer contribute to your account will one day be available for your living expenses when you retire.

Not only will the money be available; but, if you are disciplined and contribute enough money over a working career not only will the money be available but it will be more than enough to carry you through your golden years with some left over for your children.

That's the dream, the hope, the expectation.

In the process, your 401(k) Plan Provider, delicately and with an air of precision which generally dissolves any notion of further analysis, offers up software to create the illusion investing your savings can be done with no more effort than planning a trip to another continent with several cities on the itinerary.

The only difference being, a reputable online travel site will most likely get you to your destination. Sure there may be a few glitches along the way but it will get you there.

The investment software you've been given however is based on theory while the travel software is based on fact. If you book a trip to London there will be an airport, and airplanes, and ground transportation, and hotels and restaurants. Most everything you planned to do will actually be there for you to do.

Is this so with the investment software you've been given? Well, think of your money as a mode of transportation, a vehicle to get you to your destination, retirement. Any form of transportation to get you to a destination you assume will go in one direction, forward.

If you are planning a trip, your flight may get to Miami by way of Chicago; but, you usually know that before you book the flight. You are expecting it and, in turn, you are mentally prepared for it. I'm sure if you booked a direct flight and circumstances forced you to take a different flight, by way of Chicago, you would feel angry, frustrated and perhaps vow never to use the airline again.

Investment software feels like booking a direct flight.

At the risk of getting hit over the head for mentioning technical stuff, the theory driving the investment software is called the Markowitz Efficient Frontier, also known as, Modern Portfolio Theory. Harry Markowitz is now 85 years old, born in 1927 and recipient of the Nobel Prize in Economic Science and now a professor of finance at the University of California in San Diego.

Remember, this was and is theory, academic theory. Yes, it is mathematically rigorous; however, it relies on a number of assumptions around variables which must be held constant in order for it to calculate a result. The most notable variable being investment returns. In other words, the theory assumes fixed average asset returns over the spectrum of possible investment choices.

Now, I'm no rocket scientist; but, if the theory actually worked in practice, in other words, if all investment returns were 100% predictable, why wouldn't I just buy the best performing asset? Why would I bother with an efficient frontier?

Any scientist or economist analyzing the market of 2008 would have to conclude the theory failed. Assumptions about returns were blown out of the water. Assumptions about correlations, in other words the behavior of asset class returns vs. any other asset class and the degree to which they move in lock-step or move in the opposite direction also failed.

With the market of 2008 you not only missed the direct flight to Miami, you were re-routed to LA and were told the only way to get to Miami was on foot.

So, Congratulations. With the Dow and S&P now at record highs, after five years, you've made it to the East Coast, but not Miami. You're no doubt weary. You've replaced your walking shoes 10 times. You're five years older and hopefully wiser.

If you want to continue forward, it's time to do something different. Unfortunately, the consequences of ignoring all this will not be pretty because inflation isn't going away. Just saving money in cash will over time reduce your purchasing power. Basically, your money will lose value. In the future, it won't buy what it can buy today. It will buy less.

If by some form of magical thinking you're still expecting your company and the financial firm who sold your company your 401(k) will take care of you like a loving parent, I'll leave you with this.

In March of this year, two organizations hosted a 401(k) conference in Las Vegas: The National Association of Plan Advisors and the American Society of Pension Professionals & Actuaries. One of their sessions was actually titled "Heads of State" spotlighting several top broker/dealers and their views on fee compression. That's industry speak for not making as much money from your plan as they once did.

The two things which struck me as I read this article was first the arrogance, "Heads of State" ? I can think of some notorious heads of state which have ruled during my lifetime. No need to name names; and, the second point was the statement that *"as margins have compressed, no one can afford to talk to participants anymore."*

Oh by the way, the industry's new marketing buzz word to sell their products is "Retirement Readiness." Can't wait to see the marketing campaign around that one!

xoxoxo

Whose Market are You Watching

Have you been paying attention to the market lately... Have you listened on the radio or watched the News report? Do you usually watch the Financial News network on cable? How much time do you spend keeping up with the market?

The reason I mention it is the market may not be what you think. Most people have been conditioned to believe the market, as reported on news networks, has a direct relationship to their investments.

Think about it. Probably the most sited market measure mentioned in the mass media is the Dow Jones Industrial Average. That's what commentators are talking about when they say the Market fell 300 points in the first hour of trading today; or the Market closed up 100 points today; or, the market is down for the year; or the market is off it's high for the year in wild trading...

In case you didn't know, the Dow Jones Industrial Average is comprised of only 30 stocks. Yes they are generally regarded as the largest publicly traded companies out there; but, it's only 30 stocks. To put this in perspective for you there roughly 15,000 publicly traded companies in the US; about one-third are traded on the major exchanges and the rest are traded on what are called "Over the Counter" Markets.

So for you, is the Dow Jones Industrial Average important? Is it worthy of your attention? Should it's movement up or down cause you to be happy or sad? The question you may ask yourself is do you own the Dow? The short answer is... probably not.

When I've pointed this out to people over my career, they say well, there's always the S&P 500 index - that's 500 stocks. And the answer is yes, that's correct. It is 500 stocks; however, it's a bit trickier than that.

You see, the S&P 500 index is what is called market-cap-weighted. All this means is the daily impact of one stock's price change on the index is weighted by multiplying its price by the number of shares outstanding relative to the total market cap of all 500 stocks in the index. In other words, if Apple stock goes UP $20.00 the index doesn't go up 20 points. It's more like 6/10th of one point.

What that means is, the way the index works, only a handful of the largest stocks will exert the most influence on the index.

For example, the top 50 stocks (that's just 10% of the 500 stocks which make up the index) will drive over half the movement of the index on any given day. At the other end of the spectrum, if the smallest 50 stocks in the index all lost half their value in one day it would barely register in the index for the trading day.

So, if you owned the smallest 50 stocks in the index, your portfolio would lose 50% while the index may actually have been up for the day.

Does that make sense? If the Dow Jones Industrial Average is just 30 stocks and the S&P 500 index is basically 50 stocks (and oh, by the way, 21 of those 50 are also members of the Dow Jones Industrial Average) does this mean these 50 stocks will dictate the direction of the other 14,950? That's a bit silly.

Yet we all look at the Dow Jones Industrial Average and the S&P 500 index as if they have some superpowers which they don't have. We are, myself included, such creatures of habit.

The truth is if you really want to know what's happening in the market you are going to have to look to other measures.

Why? Here's the thing... the "market" not to be confused with the Dow Jones Industrial Average or the S&P 500 index, does have an influence on price movement - prices rising and prices falling. The best analogy is when the tide goes out all boats in a marina will go down. When the tide is coming in, all boats will rise. The "market" works the same way.

This is the very reason why the first question to be asked on any given day should be: Is this a market worthy of my investment capital? Why? Because you cannot enjoy rising prices in the investments you own when there are an overwhelming number of sellers in a market, any market. In Economic terms this is called "Supply." This is what happened in 2008. Most everyone was a seller.

The basic principal is: if there are more sellers willing to sell than there are buyers willing to buy, prices will fall. You see this everyday. What is the price your favorite grocer is asking for corn-on-the-cob? Is it lower than it was in November? Why? Because there are more sellers willing to sell now than there were in November. It really is that simple.

xoxoxo

Everyone Gets Fired

I want to touch on a subject which is not usually mentioned in polite society, getting fired. Fired from a job.

It's an odd attitude, if for no other reason than everyone has or knows someone who has, in fact, lost a job. It may be an entire department has been cut because of a merger or your company may decide to exit an entire business line or perhaps cutting payroll is simply a response to weak demand for whatever your company sells. The reasons are too many to list them all.

I know from personal experience about job loss because earlier in my career I lost a job after a very brief period, 5 months. Why? Simple. I chose to ignore the long term viability of the position. You see, they had a pressing need for someone to do a special project. I had the skill set needed for the assignment.

And, they couldn't tell me what I would be doing once the assignment was complete, even though I asked several times. They just said don't worry about it. And, I believed them.

The great thing about it was they paid for an outplacement service where I learned how to get a better job quicker. Really.

So what does this have to do with your 401(k)? Here's the point. Some people get fired. So why should you accept the notion that you should never sell a mutual fund in your 401(k), which is effectively firing your employee, your mutual fund money manager?

Listen, the methodology I was taught to find a better job quicker involved leveraging my existing network. Because we are not trained how to look for a job, most people will call people they know and tell them about their situation and ask if their friend has a job for them or if they know about an opening somewhere. Unfortunately, the answer is likely "no" and the conversation is over.

The methodology I was taught was to not ask for a job, it was to ask for the names of people your friends may know in companies you think you would like to join. It's a bit more involved than that; but, I've taught this simple method to many people, all of whom have used it successfully. Get in touch if you want to know more about it.

So, for me, in the process, I made well over 1,500 phone calls mostly to people I did not know but who either knew someone I knew or knew someone connected to someone I knew.

Out of all the calls I made, there was only one individual out of over fifteen hundred people who refused to help me. That's pretty impressive and also supports the statement earlier that everyone has or knows someone who has, in fact, lost a job.

All I was taught was how to help people help me and they were relieved they actually could help. I found it remarkable when I made these calls. I could feel the tension rise when I briefly explained my situation and then actually heard a sigh of relief when I told the person I wasn't calling to ask them for a job.

When I explained what kind of help I was seeking, everyone, except for the one individual I mentioned, said "Sure! I can do that." Almost everyone told me they had been through it themselves or had a friend or family member in the same position.

So, back to your 401(k)... by what form of magical thinking does Wall Street think you should hire them once (in other words, select some mutual fund or funds from the main menu of investment options) and never revisit the decision, ever again. That's what buy and hold means.

Listen, I know you know this. If you work for a company large enough to offer a 401(k), I assume you get an annual review, yes? If there are problems, they are addressed. If they are serious and continuous you may even be warned your employment is in jeopardy. If they are sudden and severe, your employer may even terminate your employment before an annual review.

So, if you are getting an annual review, shouldn't the managers you hired to invest your money get a review every so often? That's all a mutual fund is, it's a packaged product to pay someone to invest your money. You are the boss. You hired this company and you can fire them.

As the boss, it's your job to evaluate your employees. I know of no business where everything isn't measured, products, processes, services, employees, property, plant and equipment, all of it's evaluated on some fixed schedule. Even poorly managed companies are running around putting out fires, but they are putting them out.

So why not your investment managers? How are they doing? Not just the percentage return but how are they doing compared to the other investment choices you have available? And remember, cash is an investment alternative.

In many social settings, I've heard people occasionally complain about their boss. Well, here's your chance to be the boss, the boss of something personal and specific, your money and your future.

Want to be the Boss? Then act like a boss. Grab your 401(k) paperwork and put your 401(k) on the hot seat. Do an employee evaluation. Fire them if you must. How do you do an evaluation? The tools are in this book. We'll cover them in PART SEVEN.

xoxoxo

Headline Risk

One of the things I have learned over decades in the investment arena is to keep things in their true perspective.

99

For the uninformed, one of the primary risks to investing is called Headline Risk. It's the risk of being easily influenced by news headlines. Remember, in the investment arena news is not important, how the market and specifically how your investment respond to the news, is what's important.

Think about it, in October of 2013, the mass media along with the financial media had been screaming at the top of their lungs that the Government Shutdown would destroy your 401(k).

Oddly enough, or not, the technical view of the market simply did not support the rhetoric. The news cycle was focused on the idea that the Debt Ceiling Stalemate would destroy your 401(k). Again, at the time this was "Breaking News," the technical analysis did not support the rhetoric. Yet, without a method for measuring what is happening, it was easy to fall into the Headline Risk trap.

I monitor a number of keywords on my twitter feed and I saw people say they were going to move their 401(k) portfolio into the money market option until this blows over. I saw some insist that the shutdown will cost retirees money. Granted some of these tweets were pushing a political agenda. The secret behind these politically motivated headlines is they want you to believe the shutdown slash Debt Ceiling Stalemate would crush your 401(k).

However, If there is any advice I can pass along today it is this: Leave your personal politics OUT of your investment decisions. No one can predict how or when the current situation in Washington will effect your 401(k). What you can do is measure and observe what has actually happened, day-by-day, with the investments you do have in your retirement plan. Given the facts you can make intelligent choices to either stay the course or make some adjustment.

Again, perspective. At the time, the broader scope, technical analysis suggested we were in a bull market and had been for some time. Equity markets had been rising and in fact, continued to rise. How long will this last? I have no idea.

Experience suggests the market will give ample opportunities to exit when the guests begin to leave the party. It's all in the data and the data is there for anyone who looks. No one can hide it from you.

The media is very good at selling "Dog House for Sale." You all know this. Just go back a short period of time: In the summer of 2013 we were supposed to be fearful of the Fed tapering the massive bond buying program called

Quantitative Easing. That didn't stop the bull market.

Then we were supposed to be worried about the Affordable Care Act. The Debt Ceiling issue had already happened once before and the stock market has been resilient. If you've been unknowingly influenced by Headline Risk, it is no wonder you hate this bull market. You're not alone.

The only people who've been in the Dog House are the ones who have believed the story the media has been selling. Otherwise, it has been a pretty orderly uptrend in a bull market.

Again, unless you have no idea how your retirement savings are invested or how those investment choices rank in the current environment, there's been no circus and the monkeys have been safely in their cages. For those who are honestly tweeting their personal 401(k) had been hit by the Government Shutdown slash Debt Ceiling stalemate all I can say is it's time to try something different.

I must confess, I did reply to one of those Shutdown Apocalypse tweets and began it with "politics aside" and the author then replied "Does Wall Street operate politics aside? the GOP ShutDown will cost Retirees money", what I said next was, "Throughout history RELYING on Wall Street has always cost retirees. Wall Street no longer has a monopoly on information." Funny he had no response to that one.

xoxoxo

Unintended Consequences

Another perspective which may help you understand Headline Risk is that of the Mass Media. The fact is everyone loves a story. We go out of our way to hear a story. And the media is all to ready to give us what we want.

The unintended consequence I've heard surrounding inflammatory headlines is plan participants believe they are a valid reason for not saving or investing in a retirement plan.

Guess what? It's all just stories. Very well crafted, focused stories because we do love drama. How much do we love it? One way to measure is to look at the Top-Grossing Movie Genres from 1995 to 2012. The top four movie genres (out of fourteen) account for about 78% of the total market share. Know what they are? Comedy, Adventure, Drama and Action. Add the Thriller/suspense genre and we are up to 86%!

What's the point? Well, the point is, clearly, we love our emotional triggers. I remember hearing in a college marketing class there are only six emotional triggers marketing experts use to get their message across: Anger, disgust, fear, happiness, sadness and surprise. Four out of the six are negative emotion and one can go either way. Clearly, the media can grab more viewers, if they stick with the negative emotions. The consequence for you is, you just get stuck.

Make no mistake, I'm not suggesting you should be invested at all times and in all markets. What I will suggest to you is saving and a consistent plan of savings is something you can and should do at all times and in all markets.

Without savings to work with, investing and investment returns are a theoretical exercise at best. If you want gaming theory, there are better ways to occupy your time. If you are talking about your serious money then you're in the right place.

There are times when investing in cash is a good idea. But, not all the time. And being scared out of the investment market altogether because of some story in the news is just silly. Never before has it been easier to really see what is happening in the markets and with your own investments. That being said, I'll tell you there is no perfect way to manage a portfolio. Even full-time professionals disagree how to do it.

But, here are some simple guidelines for you:

The first is good diversification. Know that diversification and asset allocation are commonly confused. Diversification simply means not putting all your eggs in one basket. If you are looking at the main menu of investment options on your plan there will usually be a selection of mutual funds.

You generally don't need more than three. Each fund itself will hold a sufficient number of individual stocks or bonds which will give you immediate diversification; and, the argument can be made that one fund is all you need. However, holding more than one relieves you of the risk of style drift and the risk of a change in portfolio managers which may make the funds long term performance numbers useless.

The other simple guideline is to use relative performance when selecting from your investment options. Particularly relative to a market index like the S&P 500 as well as relative to cash. Yes, there are times when cash will outperform stock and bond investments. Unless you are measuring the relative performance of these assets on a regular basis, you will miss the signs and may fall prey to the default negative emotions the financial media is selling.

Emotional investing may make you feel better because you think you are protecting yourself; but, the outcomes rarely match the reality. Said another way, you may well be leaving money on the table, lots and lots of money, particularly over an entire working career.

xoxoxo

The Overdose Risk

Over Diversification. Yes, you can OD on diversification. Just like many prescription drugs, taking more than the minimum effective dose can have a negative effect.

Diversification, in terms of portfolio construction, is a method to manage a specific risk, the risk that one stock may result in a catastrophic loss. If 100% of your investment had been in Enron stock, you would be penniless. The point is if you spread your investment capital across several investments, the loss of any one will not leave you destitute.

It's no surprise therefore, that most plans limit the investment choices of participants to a predetermined universe of mutual funds. Remember, mutual funds and exchange traded funds are a diversified portfolio. You are not buying one stock. You are buying a basket of stocks or bonds or whatever the investment focus of the fund is.

The issue of over diversification comes into play when a 401(k) investor has too many funds. There is a downside to over diversification which I'll cover in a moment. So back to the company specific risk, the question is how many stocks is too many?   .

I seem to remember seeing a report in the 1980s which suggested 10 to 12 stocks would be all you needed to cover 90 + percent of company specific risk. I found a more recent discussion published in Barron's written by Lauren R. Rublin on April 13th, 1998, titled "Just Concentrate. Does minding fewer stocks add more oomph to a portfolio?"

The article quotes one institutional money manager who stated "The guys buying 90 to 100 stocks really are closet indexers. They're simply trying to keep up with a benchmark." Another institutional money manager quoted in the article says "Academic and industry studies have shown that the inclusion of as

103

few as 16 stocks in a portfolio eliminates as much as 93% of stock-specific risk..."

He goes on to say... and I think this is a brilliant observation... "A lot of traditional shops don't concentrate because it means taking a lot of risk to the mother ship, and major blowups can mean the end of marketing. If they don't do anything wrong, money is going to pile into their funds, even if they're just mediocre. We think diversification is a recipe for mediocrity, especially if you measure the fees of a diversified portfolio against an S&P index fund."

Now, granted, this was in 1998; however, this is the point for 401(k) investors. Markets change. There is a time when indexing will outperform actively managed funds. If you believe we are in a market where index funds are outperforming and I'm not saying we are or are not; but, if we are, this is the downside risk of over diversification, fees.

A closet indexer, in other words an actively managed fund manager who is holding more than 100 stocks, is costing you more than an index fund. Know you are paying a premium in fees if you can buy a low cost index fund offered in your plan. However, don't let your decision to invest be driven by fees alone. There's more to it than that.

Anyway, back to the topic. Within the constraints of a 401(k) plan you may own too many funds. Perhaps the asset allocation model in your plan suggested a basket of mutual funds. I think today's discussion should give you a reason to question that idea.

Even if the fund you selected owns more than 16 stocks, you still need more than one fund in your portfolio and I'll tell you why... because you have a different risk to manage when you buy mutual funds.

You are relying on one or more humans charged with the buying and selling the investments within the fund. These are just human beings and no one is perfect. The manager may make a mistake or he or she may expose you to what is called style drift. In other words if the investment focus of the fund is Large-Cap Value, it has been known to happen that a manager starts to drift from that style, perhaps moving to small cap growth stocks because Large-Cap Value isn't working and they're trying to get a performance boost.

For those reasons, in my opinion, you need at least 3 funds perhaps 4. However, beyond four, I believe, you are overdosing on diversification. The result being, in a word, mediocrity. Mediocrity means you are leaving money on the table. I don't believe you would take money out of your pocket and throw it on the sidewalk anymore than you would let a pickpocket take your money if you knew what was happening.

Remember the instructions on your meds: Warning: take only at recommended doses. Take or use exactly as directed. Do not discontinue or skip doses unless directed by your doctor.

xoxoxo

You cannot "Opt-Out" of Risk

Up to now, we've addressed solutions to a number of risks all investors face. So, let's talk about the idea of risk-free. You see it everywhere. Satisfaction guaranteed, risk-free; 100% satisfaction guaranteed risk-free; Money back guarantee risk-free; or, just risk-free guarantee.

The retail industry has used the slogan so much, it's hard not to see it. I've even seen investment books titled Risk-Free Portfolio investing...

Why? Because it's what consumers want. We don't want to look foolish. We don't want to answer to a spouse or parent or friend who we fear will think less of us, if we make a so-called, wrong decision especially where money is involved. So the idea of risk-free is appealing because we can always change our minds.

Marketing experts created the "Risk-Free" offer to overcome this obstacle. Interestingly, the term in marketing is actually called risk reversal. It's transferring the risk from the consumer onto the vendor. I'm sure you've seen the terms: 30 day free trial, no obligation, free return shipping...

Having been around the financial services industry for quite some time, it is no surprise to me that Risk-Free and Guarantee are two words Industry regulators absolutely prohibit when it comes to financial products.

They know and financial experts know risk does exist. It cannot be destroyed. It can only be moved around usually from one party to another or it can be decreased but usually at the cost of increasing some other risk.

Think about it. You don't want to lose your money so you go to buy a Bank Certificate of Deposit because CDs have the security of FDIC insurance. While some may say they are guaranteed and generally believed to be safe... are they really? If you look carefully, I don't believe you'll see the bank call them risk-

105

free or guaranteed.

Let's say the current rate on a 1 year CD is 1% and you're ok with that return to lock up your money for 12 months. What's the risk? Well, one risk may be you find yourself needing that money before the end of the 12 month term. Suppose you choose not to take the money from the CD because you don't want to get hit with the early withdrawal penalty? Suppose you miss out on buying something you've spent years trying to find.

The CD may be an effective way to radically reduce the risk of losing your money; however, the risks you've increased are first the risk of missed alternative investments and second the loss of purchasing power because of inflation. Yes I know the government tells us we don't have any inflation; but, if you do the grocery shopping for your household like I do, you know prices are going up.

In fact, I saw the results of a recent survey which asked people just like you "What is the biggest challenge facing America today, the one that you yourself are most concerned about?"

The #1 response... the Daily cost of living is too expensive.

Anyway, if you remember only one thing from this section, listen carefully... there is no risk-free. Risk never goes away. It just changes form. You cannot opt-out of risk. You can only manage risk.

Try to think of risk as your friend because there is a relationship between risk and reward. The lower the risk, the lower the reward and the reverse is true. The secret is to manage the risk. The simple rule is let your winners run and cut your losses short.

xoxoxo

Not Your Childhood Piggy-Bank

No discussion of your retirement benefits would be complete without a discussion around borrowing from the account before you retire.

First of all, what you are thinking of borrowing is your own money. That being said, you have to have money in the account and it has to be your money. Remember, if your company is matching a portion of your contribution, that portion may be subject to a vesting schedule. Vesting simply means, the company match may not be yours all at once. It may become yours only after a number of years of employment.

Next: know that not all plans allow loans. If your plan does allow loans, there are very likely limits on the amount you can borrow. And, it is not uncommon for the administrator to place restrictions on the use of the loan, such as educational or medical expenses and certain housing costs. Other restrictions likely would include how long you can use the money and the lowest interest rate you would pay for it's use.

Every plan is different so you will have to check with the human resources department at your company and they may have to check your company's plan documents to get the particulars on everything discussed so far.

In general, you do not pay tax on the money you borrow; but, if you default on the repayment schedule it would be considered a taxable distribution from the plan and may be subject to a penalty for early withdrawal.

Repayment of the loan is excluded from the calculation of the maximum annual contribution; however, in reality, it's not really a way to contribute more than the maximum, except perhaps for the interest portion you are paying yourself.

I'm not a tax expert but I would ask one if the interest portion of the repayment is taxable because it's not a "regular" contribution into the plan. My guess is, and it's just a guess is, the repayment of the principal loan amount is not taxable but I couldn't say that with authority. Again, check with your tax advisor.

Ok, that basically covers the mechanics. Yet, I think it's worth a few moments to think about borrowing from yourself.

The first thing to consider is you are putting your nest egg in jeopardy. That is a fact. I have never come across anyone who is thinking about using borrowed money who is not enthusiastic and optimistic about their ability to repay the money.

Old school banking, and I mean really old school, had three criteria for making a loan. They were called the 3 Cs. Collateral, Capacity and Character.

To an old school banker these were the criteria they relied upon to be absolutely certain they would at least get all their money back. Collateral was some asset the bank could seize and sell to cover the loan if the borrower defaulted, Real estate, Inventory, Account Receivable, Equipment and Marketable stocks and bonds.

Capacity was your cash flow history and projections for the cash flow if it was a business loan. In other words is the borrower capable of repaying the loan.

And, finally, Character. As a general rule, character was the most important criteria to an Old School Banker and it was determined by successful prior business experience or employment history; prior experience with the lender; and, referrals by people known to the banker. In a word, trust. Did the banker trust you would go to any length to pay him back.

I remember when I was a boy, maybe ten years old, my dad told me a banker would lend you money if you could prove you didn't need it. That was Old school.

What I will say is this. The reason we got into the trouble we did in 2008 is because bankers thought they could avoid the criteria of Capacity and Character by originating loans, for a fee, packaging them and selling them in the form of bonds.

From the bankers perspective, because these loans were never intended to remain on the books of the lending institution, they were far less concerned with Capacity and Character.

Some unscrupulous bankers even encouraged borrowers to lie about their capacity to repay their loans just to get the origination fee, so called "liar loans." So clearly, if a borrower was willing to lie about their ability to repay a loan we had a Capacity and Character problem from the start.

Back to today, One of the articles I saw recently suggested people are now using their 401(k) the way they were using mortgage re-financings and home equity loans before the housing bubble burst. We know how that turned out not only for the stock market but for all homeowners. I hope we're not setting ourselves up all over again.

If there is one thing you remember, I hope it is this... when you are thinking about borrowing from your 401(k), you are borrowing from yourself. You have to judge the Collateral, Capacity and Character criteria for yourself, about yourself. Can you possibly be objective? In my opinion, it is the rare individual who can.

If you have a brilliant investment or business idea and that's the reason you are thinking about borrowing from your 401(k), go to your local community bank and go through the loan approval process. If they want to throw money at you, perhaps one idea would be to take half the money from the bank and the rest from your 401(k). Or, if they turn your loan down, perhaps that's your answer. Remember, you are dealing with your nest egg. So, be careful.

xoxoxo

The Common Sense Principal of Investing

Some of you may know I grew up not too far from the Jersey Shore. We joked the Ocean was just a 15 min drive in the winter-time and about 35 min to an hour in the summer. I've always loved the Ocean, being in it, around it and near it; but, for whatever reason, I was never attracted to surfing.

However, I love to watch surfing... I've got great admiration for anyone who can glide on a stick floating in the water. The really good surfers are physically fit. It's a testament to how the human body responds to physical conditioning.

Then there's the image of sun and surf and clear water and the look of absolute joy when they catch a wave and ride it all the way... Beautiful people, beautiful locations, beautiful weather. Perfection... At least, that's the image.

The reality is quite different. Up before dawn. Cold water. Waiting. Looking. Studying wave sets. Studying how and when they break. Picking a spot. Paddling to get out there. More waiting. Watching. Choosing when to attack a wave and attacking. No fear. Getting Crushed. Struggling in the underwater turbulence. Fighting to get topside. Breaking the surface and gasping for air. Hoping the next wave in the set isn't poised to crash on your head. And the cycle repeats... in the hopes of catching the perfect wave.

What's the point of the surfing story? What's this have to do with your 401(k)?

The point is this: investing is like surfing in this regard... past performance does not predict future results. There is a process to follow... all of which is designed to stack the odds of success clearly in your favor. Conditions outside your control will influence outcomes.

The best you can hope to do is watch and wait, pick your spot and act when conditions look right. What you have here are principals of investing which most of your friends don't have. And this is critical for your success because... *principals beat theories.*

Think about it. Principals are true anywhere at anytime under any circumstances.

Principals are true regardless of who, personally, is involved. Principals are not temporarily suspended for an individual's convenience. They are universal. Some examples... Water seeks its own level; matter expands when it is heated; the angles of any triangle always add up to 180 degrees. These principals are always true. It makes no difference what country they are in, who owns them or for what purpose they're being used.

The principle being introduced to you here is the law of supply and demand. If there are more buyers willing to buy than there are sellers willing to sell, prices will rise. If there are more sellers willing to sell than there are buyers willing to buy prices will fall. It doesn't matter who the buyers or sellers are. It doesn't matter where they live. It doesn't matter how rich or poor they are, what they drive, married, single, childless or not. The Laws of Supply and demand work. They are not a theory.

In contrast, the investing Theories of Buy and Hold, Asset Allocation Strategy, Modern Portfolio Theory and the Efficient Frontier are just theories. How do we know? Because history has demonstrated, even in the recent past, they do not work at all times and in all markets. Remember, a Principal is true anywhere, at anytime, under any circumstances.

The tools to follow will help you see, with your own eyes, when demand is in control or when supply is in control.

xoxoxo

The News is Bad

Sample news headlines:
Global Shares, Oil Rebound but Growth Worries Linger
Gold Up in Roller-coaster Trade, nerves still on edge.
Gold Could Head Much Lower
Warning to France: 'Time is Running Out'
Emerging Stocks Decline to Five Month Low as Commodities Slump

Ok, now. How are you feeling? Concerned? Anxious? Fearful? Satisfied? Hungry for more?

Some time ago I saw an online article in The Guardian, a UK newspaper, titled:

News is bad for you, and giving up reading it will make you happier. It's an edited extract from an essay first published at dobelli.com. The Art of Thinking Clearly: Better Thinking, Better Decisions by Rolf Dobelli.

I want to share this with you because I believe this will benefit you not only regarding your 401(k), but your investments, and life, in general. The sub-headlines of the article are as follows:

News Misleads
News is Irrelevant
News has no Explanatory Power
News is Toxic to your body
News increases cognitive errors.
News inhibits Thinking
News works like a drug
News wastes time
News makes us Passive
News Kills Creativity

The Author, Rolf Dobelli, opens the article comparing consumption of news to sugar, candy for the mind. Small tidbits, easy to consume, which don't really concern our lives and require no thinking on our part.

The point the author makes is that unlike books or lengthy magazine articles which require thinking, news flashes, scanning headlines, breaking news announcements can be swallowed in almost limitless quantities which is about as beneficial as mindlessly eating a pound of chocolate in half ounce servings.

So, lets think about this:

News Misleads:
What are news-borne hazards? Well, think of news as a product. The lower the cost to produce "news" the higher the profit. How much time does it take to dramatize a story vs. getting to what's relevant. Something happened, an explosion, a car crash, an airplane falls into a suburban area or the Dow drops 1,000 points.

What's the media focus? The drama, who got hurt, how many, what were they doing before it happened, where were they when it happened. All of this is relatively easy to assemble and report. To get to the causes and the likelihood of this happening in *your* life isn't cheap and can't be uncover fast enough for the normal news cycle.

What Dobelli suggests is this "news" creates a false risk map in our brains. His examples: "terrorism is over-rated. Chronic stress is under-rated. The collapse of Lehman Brothers is overrated. Fiscal irresponsibility is under-rated. Astronauts are over-rated. Nurses are under-rated."

I love his comment "We are not rational enough to be exposed to the press."

News is Irrelevant:
He asks, out of the 10,000 news stories you may have read in the last 12 months, did even one allow you to make a better decision about a serious matter in your life, your career or your business?

The underlying belief we've been spoon-fed is "news" gives us some sort of competitive advantage. With all of the technology we possess today it is easy to be connected 24/7. Smart Phones, iPads and computer tablets are really portable and we take them everywhere. (I recently heard about one company suggesting employees take cellphones with them to the restroom.)

Leaving these devices behind can now cause anxiety because we feel separated from this flow of news. I can tell you, news has never helped me make better investment decisions, in fact it has been a competitive disadvantage and I've watched it scare investment professionals into giving poor advice to their clients.

News is toxic to your body:
Panicky stories trigger chemical reactions in your body, particularly cortisol which de-regulates your immune system. Therefore, constant exposure to news puts your body in a chronic state of stress with other side effects being fear, aggression, tunnel-vision and de-sensitization.

News increases cognitive errors:
The two most hazardous errors being confirmation and story bias. Cognitive biases are patterns of thinking which may impact our emotional state and behavior and have been demonstrated by research in psychology and behavioral economics.

In the face of overwhelming news tidbits, our brain filters out anything which may challenge our prior conclusions and will gravitate to any news which confirms our decisions. The outcomes of this bias may include missed opportunities, financial losses, overconfidence or arrogance.

The story bias takes unrelated bits of information to satisfy the craving to "make sense" of things, regardless of reality. I laughed when I read Dobelli's comment that "Any journalist who writes, "The market moved because of X" or "the company went bankrupt because of Y" is an idiot."

Remember, the end of the world can only happen once.

So what can you do?

Here's a suggestion, treat news the way you treat food. You would be appalled if you watched someone eating every waking moment of the day. Put yourself on a news diet.

Start with the financial news and see how that feels. If there is some area of relevant interest, you can use Google to alert you to specific topics in the news. They'll send you an e-mail. Read books about the topic or try audio books you can consume while you drive or work-out.

Yes, you may experience some anxiety; but, you will find you can re-program the physical structure of your brain. The result of being exposed to news for so long is that the neurons inside your skull have abandoned the cells devoted to concentration, thinking with profound focus, and strengthened the ones devoted to skimming and multitasking. You may find concentration has become difficult, you tire easily and may become restless when you try it. but, it will get better.

Think of all the time you will save. Read a newspaper or watch the news every morning, grab some news at lunch, News before or after dinner, before you go to bed? Add it up and you may find yourself with 12 hours or more every week you can devote to something fun.

xoxoxo

The Fee Frenzy

For several months now the topic of Fees has been in the news. I guess it started with the PBS Frontline drama called "The Retirement Gamble" and more recently fueled by the reaction to a Yale professor who sent out around 6,000 letters to select employers with 401(k) plans warning they are paying too much and suggesting they take steps to face their responsibilities, or else...

The frenzy came center stage because of the perception the letters were threatening. He said he would name names. One source quoted the letter as

113

saying

Quote "We will make our results available to newspapers (including the New York Times and the Wall Street Journal) as well as disseminate the results via Twitter with a separate hashtag for your company." Close Quote.

I guess that got attention because there was an almost immediate talk of lawsuits.

Follow-up articles went into discussing the flaws in the professors' research and who may be named in a lawsuit. Drama. Lots and lots of drama...

So what's the point? How's this relevant to your 401(k)?

Here's the thing: Fees are an easy target for everyone to take a shot at. It's easy to get everyone polarized. Vanguard has made a fortune selling low fees the same way Wal-Mart has made a fortune selling lowest prices. In principal, no one wants to pay high fees. I know I don't. But, what we are talking about here is not the same as buying food, shelter or clothing.

What we're talking about is a service, an ongoing service. Yes, it is packaged and sold as a product; but, it's actually a service. What we are talking about is ongoing management of your investments. You may choose to buy an investment in your 401(k) and forget it; but, whether it is a so called index fund or an actively managed portfolio, those assets are managed 365 days a year.

Are fees important? Sure they are. However, what should be more important to you is the net return. Think about it, would you like an actively managed mutual fund which brought home a 25% return year to date or an index which brought home a 19% return?

The index is cheaper; but, the reported returns are net of fees. "Net of Fees" simply means all the fees are deducted before the calculation of the return. Who wouldn't want the 25% return net of fees?

So why all this attention on fees?

Well, think about it. Depending on your age, you may remember the government has on a number of occasions tried price controls, They didn't work. The government mandated 401(k) plans to report fees to employees. Is this a first step in increasing regulation of the industry? I have no idea.

Am I saying it's foolish to tell you what you are paying in 401(k) fees? No. I'm not. You should know what fees you are paying and more to the point you should know you *are* paying fees. Should fees be the sole factor in deciding which investments to pick. Absolutely not! Net returns are what's important to you.

Ok. So why would the media care about reporting on fees. Well, fees are great for news reporting, again because it's dramatic. It's easy to get people inflamed over high fees because no one, particularly in this economy, wants to pay high fees. And, it's easy to report that a fee is high just by looking at the numbers, in isolation; but, again, is this a high fee problem or a low value problem.

Back to our example, if the fees for the actively managed mutual fund were 2.75% while the fees for the index fund were only 0.07%, the fee question is this. Is the 2.75% fee high? In isolation, sure it is. Is it a better value for the investor? Sure it is. Should I resent paying the 2.75% fee? You're welcome to; however, I'd be happy to pay that fee all day long for the superior return.

Remember, the 2.75% fee is deducted *before* the return is calculated.

What's ironic is by keeping a focus on fees we keep the focus *off* what's important, returns. Is the idea to keep you from focusing on the almost non-existent returns over the last 13 years because the industry has successfully sold you on the idea of buy-and-hold? Riding markets up only to ride them back down again?

How does the focus on fees keep you from what should *always* be your primary focus, investment returns? Think about it. Does the discussion of fees make you feel powerless? Clearly you as an individual have no control over what funds are selected for your plan and in turn if the investments selected have high or low fees.

Does the discussion of fees make you feel angry or resentful? I'd be surprised if they don't. But know this, these are emotions which do not serve you in the management of your money.

The biggest criticism and potentially the most damaging result of the PBS Frontline drama called "The Retirement Gamble" was the producers made an *editorial* decision to shock the audience. Some say they went too far and may well have frightened people so severely they began asking if it even made sense to put money into a 401(k).

Rather than feeling powerless or angry or resentful over fees why not channel that energy into what will make a difference, measuring the price movement of the investments which are available in your plan. How about looking at the relative strength of the investments to see which are the strongest performers in your plan.

These are actions which will get you a better return for a small amount of effort. At the end of the day, it is the return on your investments which will get you a comfortable retirement. Provided of course, you save enough money to grow along the way.

xoxoxo

When Fees Are a Big Deal

Let's explore the fee issue just a bit further. For some time now I've been thinking about the Index fund vs. actively managed mutual fund debate which has been going on recently. Well, actually, it's been around for as long as I've been in the business and there are vocal fans on both sides of the table.

The loudest argument made by the Index fund camp, is low fees; but, in my experience, this is only appealing to the individual investor when no one is making money. In other words, in the absence of VALUE the only thing left to discuss is price. I never heard the argument when the market was on fire during the mid 80's or during the dot com rage or in 2007, just before the liquidity crisis.

If everyone is making money, no one cares about fees, it's a non-issue. Fees only become a hot-button in the absence of value creation. And, isn't that what you want from a money manager? If no one is focused on avoiding catastrophic losses because they are selling buy-and-hold, insisting you ride markets up only to ride them back down again, over a decade of *experience* tells you there *is* no value, so why should you pay for that?

The Index camp is quick to say that historically the majority of actively managed mutual funds fail to do at least as well as an index fund. This seems to be the primary argument yet I've never seen more detail given.

So, what got me thinking is this. Ok, suppose this statement is true? What *majority* number are we talking about here? Is it 51% 75% or 99%?

If it's less than 100% then relative strength analysis will point you to those managers who ARE outperforming the index. Remember, return numbers have to be reported *after* fees have been deducted. My thinking is... if they're delivering performance numbers greater than the index, there is little reason to obsess about fees.

So I started my research to see what the numbers really look like. What I found is a piece of research titled the S&P INDICES VERSUS ACTIVE FUNDS SCORECARD The registered trade-name being SPIVA.

You can download it from US.SPINDICES.COM

Download the PDF if you want to follow along, look at page three, the table titled ANNUAL LEAGUE TABLES OVER THE PAST 10 YEARS, EXHIBIT ONE.

Using their numbers for ALL Large Cap Funds vs. the S&P 500 index, the 10 year average is 59.6%. In other words, 59.6% of actively managed funds *underperformed* the S&P 500 index. (remember the authors of this research are reporting on the benefit of Index funds) The High being 81.28% in 2011 and the Low being 44.5% in 2005.

Drilling down a little deeper, isolating the Large Cap CORE Funds vs. the S&P 500 index the 10 year average is 60.8%. The High being 81.31% again in 2011 and the Low being 44% in 2007. Again, All these numbers represent the percent of actively managed funds which *underperformed* their index benchmark

Now looking at the Mid-Cap CORE Funds vs. the S&P MidCap 400 index the 10 year average is 63.1% *underperformed*. The High being 82% in 2010 and the Low being 35.9% in 2006.

Finally looking at the Small-Cap CORE Funds vs. the S&P SmallCap 600 index the 10 year average is 62.4% *underperformed*. The High being 86% in 2011 and the Low being 33.3% in 2003.

Now, let's look at it in reverse, just subtracting the numbers above from 100%, the 10 year average of Actively Managed Mutual Funds *Outperforming* their respective index in the following categories were as follows:

ALL Large Cap Funds, 40.4%
Large Cap CORE Funds, 39.2%
Mid-Cap CORE Funds, 36.9% AND
Small-Cap CORE Funds, 37.6%

For me, what the *year by year data* shows is that Indexing is not a hands down winning strategy at all times and in all markets. Markets are dynamic. Things change. No one can predict the changes.

Again, for me, what the *10 year average data* shows is there *has* been better than one third of actively managed mutual funds which *have* historically *outperformed* their index benchmarks.

Let's be clear here, the point is not to advocate for or against Index funds or for or against actively managed mutual funds. The point is if you don't know where the relative strength is and you take the "easy" way out, you will likely leave money on the table, or worse, you may even lose money.

I was talking with a friend the other day and he mentioned a number of his co-workers have said "boy, I love it since they introduced those target date funds! I just don't have to worry about it anymore!!!"

Just know, the Chairman of the Federal Reserve Bank will eventually begin to "taper" the quantitative easing program that has pushed interest rates down and stock prices up. Once that happens there will likely be a spike in interest rates and owners of Target Date funds will likely see their account values drop if only because of the bond portion of the portfolio.

Especially hard hit will be those workers closest to retirement who own these so called *easy* investments. Why? Because they will have the largest proportion of their target date fund portfolio allocated to bond market investments. If interest rates go up, bond prices go down.

Those closest to retirement age will have two particular challenges to face. First they will not have much time to recover losses on the bond portfolio which can arguably only come from income and second it is unlikely interest rates will fall again, in a timely manner, to reverse the losses.

Target Date Fund managers have been known to move down the credit quality scale taking on Junk Bonds to increase yield before. I'm sure that will be tempting if bond values crash.

Anyway, the suggestion for today is quit now. Quit looking for the easy way out. You may think you don't have to worry about your retirement investments today; but, just know, this is not a rehearsal.

You will not get a chance to do it over when you've finished your working career and are stepping into retirement. The safest investment you can ever make is your own education because no one can ever take that away from you.

xoxoxo

Blind Faith

You probably know me well enough by now to know I love words. I've heard it said the English language can be difficult for some people to learn because we sometimes attach very different meanings to the same word. In the process, we may fail to really communicate because two or more people directly involved in a conversation may come away with completely different understandings. Sometimes intentionally. Sometimes not.

In the area of 401(k) investment advice, from the provider of your company retirement plan, there may be similarities.

Let me explain: This morning I saw an article by Andrea Coombes on the Wall Street Journal's Online Channel called Market Watch. The title: 401(k) investment advice: Can you trust it?

The basis of Andrea's article is a new survey by the AARP, the group which advocates for older Americans. In turn, the AARP survey addresses an issue which is currently being considered by The U.S. Department of Labor: namely re-defining what the term "fiduciary" means in relation to advice given regarding retirement plans.

What's the point? What's this have to do with you? Quite a bit, actually. The discussion around getting advice from a Fiduciary or not has direct bearing on whether or not your 401(k) provider or possibly your employer are legally responsible, if the advice you take results in your losing money. The whole discussion here has to do with who is responsible because when it comes to your money you need to know who is responsible.

Before we go any further, Let's back up a step because the first piece of the puzzle is what is advice? Everything communicated to you about your retirement plan does not necessarily count as advice from a legal standpoint.

Information presented on your plan's website and even what may be said during an in-house, 401(k) seminar does not rise to the level of advice. Those are considered forms of guidance or education from a legal point of view rather than advice.

The point being, if no one gave you advice, you and you alone are responsible.

From a legal perspective, advice typically occurs when someone tells you, personally, one-on-one, how you should invest your money: What to buy, how much to buy and perhaps when to buy it.

In addition, it is not a one-time event. This instruction of what to buy, how much, and when will be continuous. As a general rule, If it isn't personal and specific and continuous, it doesn't rise to the standard of advice and the issue of Fiduciary isn't relevant.

If you invest based on a computer model generating a pie-chart, this is not advice.

So, moving on to the standard of Fiduciary. To make this easy for you, in general, a Fiduciary must only give advice which is in the best interest of the person being given the advice. It may come as a shock to you to discover the advice you think you are getting, first of all, is not actually advice; and, secondly, may not be *entirely* in your best interest.

When it comes to retirement plans the vendor hired by your company to provide the 401(k) platform may be a broker/dealer or a registered investment advisor. In general, registered investment advisors are held to the standard of Fiduciary while a broker-dealer generally is not.

I know this is confusing because you probably don't know the difference. So here is the single best tip for you.

Ask. Don't ask Human Resources or anyone else in your company because they may not know the difference either. Ask the representative *from* the 401(k) you're talking to, If you aren't talking with someone person-to-person, whatever information you may be basing your investment decision on, probably isn't advice. If you are talking *with* a representative FROM the 401(k), ask directly "Are you acting as a fiduciary?" By the way: it's a yes or no question and there is only a yes or no answer. Insist on an answer.

If they say no, then they are operating from a less stringent standard of advice called "Suitability." In other words the advice they give you must be suitable for you given your situation. Be aware a recommendation may be given to you which will result in a higher payout to the person giving the advice vs. another product *and* according to the standard, it may still be judged Suitable.

Make no mistake, I've operated in both worlds and I personally know of very few broker/dealer representatives who have had a *total* disregard for the people they are advising.

Those people are usually found out by their clients or the broker/dealer and don't last long in the business. So, if someone tells you they are not a fiduciary just be aware. It doesn't mean you should not believe what they tell you. However, that being said, you can certainly ask them to tell you how they are getting paid and to explain the different fees involved in the products they're recommending vs. the other choices available.

Now if that is not confusing enough there is one more wrinkle. Remember the discussions we've had about Target Date Funds, particularly in retirement plans where this product is the default investment option? In other words, unless you yourself make a change, your contributions and your company's matching contributions will automatically be invested in this product. It's the default. Do nothing and this will be your retirement investment vehicle. OK?

The Fiduciary Standard is especially important for you. Why? Because Target Date Funds are specifically exempt from the fiduciary standard when the plan is designed with them as the default investment.

Said another way, neither your company nor the vendor your company hired to provide the 401(k) plan can be held liable by you if the investment does not perform as expected.

They cannot be sued if you lose money simply because you believed them when they offered a broadly diversified portfolio which relieves you of the responsibility of periodic rebalancing. So if you are holding on to the idea that your company is responsible for the investment performance of this product because they picked it for you, you've just been warned. They are not. You and you alone are responsible. Period. End of story.

xoxoxo

Write it Down

Years ago, I received a bit of of wisdom which I'll share with you. Write down your ruling reason for buying an investment. That way you will have, in black and white, the reason to sell the same investment because the ruling reason will either prove correct, or not.

Let me give you an example. I had a client years ago, a partner in a national law firm. His area of practice was securities law. I met him when I was an investment banker. Anyway, he called me one day and told me he wanted to buy a thousand shares of a bank headquartered here in town.

I thought it was a curious request so I asked him what was his ruling reason. He said he'd spent years now watching national banks buying up regional banks in the State and figured this particular bank had to be on someone's hit list and he'd eventually make 50% on his money.

I said ok. Got him the shares and forgot about it. About 18 months later, a press release was issued by the bank that the Board of Directors had approved a buy-out offer made by a national bank in a stock for stock exchange.

I called my client with congratulations and told him I could put in a limit order to sell his shares which were now trading at a 60% premium from his purchase price. He said no, no, no. I don't want to sell! Surprised, I asked why!? Your ruling reason for buying the shares was in anticipation of a buy-out. You were right. So, what's the ruling reason for owning shares in this new bank? What do you know about it? He said, "I don't know anything about them. I just don't want to pay the tax on the gain!"

We talked a little more. I showed him the chart on the new bank. (which didn't look all that impressive) But, his mind was made up. As it turned out, the shares of the new bank continued to drift lower and his 60% premium evaporated. He ended up selling the position a few years later at a loss.

The point here is, with a ruling reason, you can *objectively* make investment decisions, leaving emotions out of the equation, because it has been well documented that emotional investment decisions rarely work.

Without a ruling reason *and* a logical organized systematic approach to investing it is just too easy to fall into human defense mechanisms as to why you should hold on to losing investments.

Ever make these mistakes?

How about Displacement? Discharging pent-up feelings, usually of hostility, on objects less dangerous than those which initially aroused the emotion: Example: You are continuing to hope a losing investment will turn around, so you sell one which has a small profit just to make yourself feel smart (only to have the losing position continue to lose more money while the one you sold continues to go up in price.)

122

How about Rationalization? Justifying one's failures with socially acceptable reasons instead of the real reasons. Example: After the bubble burst in 2008 you told friends and family the reason you lost so much money in your 401(k) was because of the crooks on Wall Street. The real reason you lost money was because you didn't take the time to adopt a logical organized systematic approach to managing your money.

How about Denial? Refusing to admit something unpleasant is happening. Example: Taking your 401(k) account statements and filing them, unopened, because you are afraid you are losing money and don't know what to do about it.

All of these responses can be overcome when you have a ruling reason and a systematic approach to investing your 401(k). Vigilance is a small price to pay for your future. The great thing is, vigilance doesn't have to mean being on constant guard obsessively looking for financial news reports to charge your emotions.

Vigilance can be nothing more than checking the charts and relative strength rankings of your investment options on a fixed time schedule, preferably with the TV off and the stock market closed.

In these quiet moments, because it takes only a few minutes, you can see clearly what is and then make a rational, logical decision to buy, sell or hold. That's all you ever have to do. Simple. No drama.

You don't need to run to Morningstar and compile columns of numbers or wait for them to add or subtract a Star, revising their rating after the fact, causing you to miss an opportunity because the price has already moved before they revised their opinion.

Remember: Selling your winning investments and waiting for your losers to come back is like cutting down the rose bushes and watering the weeds.

xoxoxo

The Buddhist Key to Investing

What can be done to help people save?

I consider myself a lifelong learner and one of my interests is the human brain and how it works. I was fascinated when I discovered the Charlie Rose Brain

Series. You can find it online if you're interested. I find this fascinating because I have seen first hand how investors respond to perceived risk and reward; and, I am fascinated how these responses are now being mapped in the brain, right up to the point of digital imaging. Very cool.

Another area of personal interest has always been spirituality and spiritual practices across various cultures. This is not something new for me. My family was mildly curious when, before the age of 20, I studied Transcendental Meditation and practiced TM for quite a few years. I still use it on occasion.

Now a few weeks ago, I was really intrigued when I found something I've never seen before which is a collaborative effort between these two fields. What I discovered was there has been an annual conference sponsored by what is called The Mind & Life Institute which has been held now for the past 27 years.

The Mind & Life Institute began as an intellectual experiment between His Holiness the 14th Dalai Lama, entrepreneur R. Adam Engle, and neuroscientist Francisco J. Varela.

It's a non-profit organization that seeks to understand the human mind. Ultimately, their goal is to relieve human suffering and advance well-being. The most recent conference focuses its attention on craving, desire, and addiction, as these are among the most pressing causes of human suffering. You can find it at www.mindandlife.org.

I am getting to what this has to do with your 401(k), really.

One of the Presenters at the conference, the morning of the Fourth day, on October 31st, was one Matthieu Ricard, Ph.D. who is also a practicing Tibetan Buddhist Monk. His contribution was titled: From Craving to Freedom and Flourishing: Buddhist Perspectives on Desire. (see 25:35)

What fascinated me was the discussion around when is it possible to administer an antidote to suffering. The Buddhist phrase he used was "managing with skillful means," to break the pattern of suffering. What we're talking about are overpowering emotions. And these are the same emotions which make us such poor investors and in my opinion poor savers.

In the beginning we're not prepared. While it is happening, we are swept up and overpowered; and, after the fact, we experience anger and frustration. So according to Matthieu the place to begin is **after** by investigating the causes and consequences which got us in our present condition. How did I get in this mess?

After, we may first experience regret; however, regret in this context is not guilt. It's only a recognition of how this happened. I don't like this condition. So, why should I repeat this pattern? In turn, we may need to seek support; apply an antidote and then make a pledge not to repeat the behaviors which got me in this mess in the first place.

So the first part is how does this apply to saving and your 401(k)? Well, if we yield to our human cravings and desires and fail to look to the future, we will not have the freedom to stop working for money at normal retirement age. We will be slaves. If we are physically or mentally unable to continue working at normal retirement age because we have not prepared, we may be worse than slaves.

So the issue of responding to our mess after the fact as Matthieu suggests really won't work when it comes to saving for retirement because there is no more time for corrective behavior. After is too late. So as I said from the beginning, the number one task for you is to actually save and to do so as early as possible.

What tools can we use? One of the most powerful tools available is imaginings. Imaginings of positive experiences as an aid to motivation when it comes to saving and also investing.

So perhaps what may work for you is to imagine, in an almost a dream like state, how you would envision your retirement years. Take the time to dream. What kind of life would you like to have for yourself?

We are dreaming so go ahead and picture the life you want to create for yourself. Where would you like to live? Be specific. Paint a detailed picture. Go to Pinterest and look for images that appeal to you.

What would your housing look like? How will it look and feel? Can you think of what sights and smells you will experience in this place? Will it be in a forest or mountain or on the coast? What forms of entertainment will be nearby? What passions would you like to pursue in retirement. Who are you with? What are you doing?

Now, begin to put a foundation under that dream to make it real. View it as a destination at the end of a train ride and reverse engineer how you will get there.

There are free retirement calculators online. Use them. And, use your dream to fall back on when you are thinking you don't want to save or are tempted to raid your 401(k) for something frivolous today.

Now, when it comes to investing, I believe, Matthieu's strategy **is** applicable. We've already experienced two catastrophic market environments which have made a mess of your investments.

The tools discussed in this book offer an antidote for you to break the pattern. You just need to make a pledge not to repeat the old investment strategies which have failed on the promise to get you to your dream. It is simple. It will take a bit of effort; but, it's simple. Keep your eye on the prize! Your dreams depend on it.

xoxoxo

Trash Talk

One of my sources of personal inspiration is an author by the name of Seth Godin. His area of expertise is marketing; but, he often comes up with some interesting insights into human behavior. His latest post was titled "Trash Talking Important Work."

What's this have to do with your 401(k)? I'll tell you. You know I follow a number of key words on my twitter feed. And, it amazes me how many tweets are just that: Trash talk.

Some examples:
"Don't worry about retirement money. The Regime will confiscate all the 401(k)'s."

Another:
"401(k)? No thanks! I ran a 5k once and almost puked."

OR
"That 401(k) will bounce up & down like a yo-yo & money managers spend that money. $1 today may be worth a dime later."

Or
"I didn't sign up for the 401(k) at work, because there's no way I can run that far."

OR
"I want a friend with benefits, dental & medical insurance, 401(k) retirement

plan, etc.

If you don't believe me, just type in 401(k) into the twitter search bar. You'll see similar trash talk. It's sarcasm. Look up the word sarcasm in the dictionary and you will find the word comes from the Greek meaning literally "to tear flesh." I can think of nothing more violent than that.

So why do people talk this way about their retirement planning? Call it a coping mechanism. Seth suggests (and this is important) it's a *self*-induced anxiety formula. He describes the self talk this way:

What I'm about to do is important. I've never done it quite like this. It's incredibly crucial, a turning point, a high risk venture, a moment in time I won't have again. Therefore, I am nervous. And I need to get *more* nervous, because the *importance* of the moment warrants it. This is going to *fail*. I can vividly *picture* all the ways it won't work...

And, because there is so much anxiety and confusion around this topic we do one thing, we minimize the event. Again in Seth's words:

The mantra is: No one will be watching. I'm exaggerating this moment. It's no big deal. It's not as important as you think. It doesn't really matter...

It's this type of thought process which creates the Tweets I just mentioned. Basically, we tell ourselves it *doesn't really matter* and we go on to craft a *story* to justify this type of thinking *and* why we needn't bother with it.

I've heard it said that we are the sum total of all the choices and decisions we have made up to this point. Choices have consequences. How we feel about consequences, being right or wrong or good or bad is just part of the story we tell ourselves. What is gripping is we always get to make new choices and in the process get to experience new consequences.

Accepting, without judgement, where we are gives us clues where we have the power to change.

If we choose, consciously or unconsciously, to spend all of our money today, more likely than not, we will become the grasshopper in one of Aesop's Fables.

It's very easy to blame advertisers and the companies which hire them to make their products unbelievably tempting. But, to be honest, it is we who open our wallets and volunteer.

To use Seth's words again. He says: "In fact, it *does* matter. In fact, this *is* an important thing you're about to do, and denigrating it undermines the very reason you're doing this work in the first place."

So here's a solution you can start today: Stop the trash talk. *Substitute* the idea that Nervous is ok. That feeling is actually *proof* that you are on to something important. You are on to something worthwhile. Something you will thank yourself for later. If you can, *embrace* the nervousness, welcome the fear. Why? Because the feeling becomes a fuel to a better life.

Just hoping things will work hasn't worked for anyone I've talked to. You have to do something different if you want something different. One bit of parting wisdom for today, what get's measured, gets done. You can measure what's happening in your 401(k).

xoxoxo

Beliefs Have Consequences

One of my all time favorite quotes is by Abraham Lincoln. He said: "Folks are usually about as happy as they make their minds up to be."

Simple truth. Happiness is a choice. Another simple truth: the biggest barrier to my happiness is usually myself. Someone told me long ago : "if you want something different, you have to DO something different."

So, if you want something different, if you want to break down barriers to making better 401(k) investment choices, let me give you a tip. I know you know this, even if you don't want to admit it. Choices have consequences. And, guess what?

"Not choosing" is, in fact, a choice. And, yes, there will be a consequence. Not right or wrong or good or bad; but, there will be a consequence which is nothing more than a natural outcome that results from a choice.

If you've watched your 401(k) get whip-sawed by the markets over the last 5 years, 10 years or even 20 years, perhaps it's time to do something different. Or, if you've never participated in your 401(k) because you say "Oh! I'm not good at that. I don't know anything about it." Then, you *are* making a choice.

Some questions you may want to ask yourself are... who is making all the decisions about how I get to invest for retirement? Who is going to determine what kind of future I am going to have? Is it just some members of Wall Street who have clearly demonstrated they are primarily concerned with their own wealth?

This combustable mix of ignorance and power, sooner or later, is likely to blow up in your face. Like it or not, investing involves a way of thinking. A way of skeptically interrogating the universe with a fine understanding of human fallibility.

If you are not able to objectively evaluate what so called experts are telling you is true, then you are up for grabs for the next Ponzi or Madoff who comes along.

The consequence of not choosing is to keep moving in the same direction you have been moving and to keep experiencing the outcomes you have been experiencing. "Not choosing" is the *belief* that a better, alternative has not been presented and it is the belief that is critical.

The gripping part of this choosing is we are usually pre-conditioned. Judgments happen long before we think they do. Usually because a belief has already been planted, subtly, which influences today's choices.

Think about the choices you make every day... Foreign or domestic food, beverages, fashion, furniture or an automobile? You have an opinion, no doubt. It's likely automatic. The interesting part is your opinion was first influenced by some primal emotion - and, then, after the fact, you substantiated it with so called facts. You believe you reasoned it out.

Now when conditions change, letting go of that old pattern becomes difficult. Why?

Because in the face of change, you may fall into the trap of black and white thinking: the notion that your earlier choice was either right or wrong. Funny how the brain works. There is another way to look at it... Suppose you assume the first choice was *right*... at the time; but conditions changed... as they always do. And what you are facing now is nothing more or less than a new choice. Entirely new.

I recall when I was a boy, the phrase "Made in China" had a judgement attached to it. It was a very negative judgement. It meant the product was cheap - very poor quality - and would not last. However you may feel about Apple products, iPods, iPhones and iPads... where are they made? China. Poor quality? Apple doesn't think so. I don't think so. And, the buyers of Apple products don't think so. "Made in China" doesn't mean what it once did. Does that mean the statement wasn't true in the 50s and 60s? No. For the most part it was true... at the time.

Remember this: change is inevitable. You only have to look in the mirror to see the truth in this statement. You are not a teen-ager anymore despite what your brain tells you.

And guess what, change is the single constant in the relative strength of your investment choices: inside your 401(k) and anywhere else you care to invest. If you look at the annual results of the top performing asset class over the last 30 years, guess what: no asset class has kept the top slot the entire time. It changes almost every year.

xoxoxo

Managing the Downside

I recently saw a quote attributed to Socrates which says: "I cannot teach anybody anything. I can only make them think."

So, let's think... together. Consider this...

On February 3rd, 2014, the major market indices were down around 2%. The S&P 500 was off 2.28; the Dow was off 2.08 and the Nasdaq was off 2.61%

What made this seem severe was we hadn't seen this kind of pullback for several months and it didn't *feel* normal. But was it? Again, Let's zoom out. We have to go back to August 16th, 2013 to find a weekly decline of over 2%.

That's 171 days ago or 342 editions of prime time morning and evening news. Now if you look back through the weekly data going to 1975, what you'll see is, on average, weekly declines of 2% or more happen about seven times a year.

Said another way, on average, 7 times a year is about once every 50 days. Remember we're talking averages here and we've mentioned the hazards of relying on averages. However, the purpose here is simply to gain some perspective.

The point is the decline was not unique and panic was not an appropriate emotional response. In my opinion, no emotional response is good when it comes to investing.

The thing to think about in these situations is what is called a stop-loss point. A stop loss is nothing more than a price at which you determine to sell an investment to preserve capital.

Personally, I don't like automatic stop-loss orders. Although for the Plan Participant this is usually not an option anyway unless you are making a trade in the self-directed brokerage account within your 401(k).

My preference is to use what I call a mental stop-loss. On any given day I may look at an investment and make a mental note of the price at which the investment has to be sold.

Discomfort and anxiety usually come into play when that price is reached because there is always the nagging thought that you may be wrong. The market may reverse and you will leave money on the table.

So, the important thing about executing a stop-loss is deciding, beforehand, to live with the stop-loss regardless of where the price goes from there. Remember, the purpose of the stop-loss is preservation of capital. A wise friend told me once, you cannot control the market. You are responsible for the effort, not the outcome. But, preservation of capital gives you the ability to choose again.

Lose all your money and you don't have many choices.

xoxoxo

Inevitable Boom and Bust

On July 24th, 2014, I saw an interview of the Former Federal Reserve Chairman, Alan Greenspan. He's now 88 years old.

Alan Greenspan served five terms as chairman of the Board of Governors of the Federal Reserve System. He was appointed chairman by four different presidents. He received his bachelor's, master's, and doctoral degrees in economics, all from New York University.

And, it seems, in light of the financial crisis in 2008, he has been focusing his powerful intellect on human nature which he distilled in his recent book, "The Map and the Territory."

The interview, last week, focused on his views of the Federal Reserve dilemma of how to unwind the huge increase in the size of its balance sheet and how to address stock market and other asset bubbles.

What caught my attention in the interview and the reason I got so excited was Mr. Greenspan's conclusion was that bubbles are a function of human nature; and, his current belief that it is unrealistic for central banks to think they can stop them.

My initial impression of the interview was *finally*... an irrefutable, authoritative source which will herald the end of the Buy-and-hold dogma which has caused so much anguish in your quest to secure a comfortable retirement.

Looking at a number of Book Reviews just to get a peek into "The Map and the Territory," it seems Mr. Greenspan is of a mind that we should be able to build human nature into our economic forecasting models and predict future crashes.

He is an economist after all; and, has spent his career, inside and outside of government, contributing to economic *models* to understand the economic landscape and *predict* outcomes.

Of note, Mr. Greenspan also identifies "too big to fail" as the most problematic trend emerging from 2008. He sees government expenditures on companies deemed "too big to fail," ...their rescue, as a slippery slope to favoritism and state ownership.

All that's fascinating to me; however, the point here is to take to heart his epiphany that central banks are powerless to control asset bubbles.

Mr. Greenspan states in the interview, and I quote: "When bubbles emerge, they take on a life of their own. It is very difficult to stop them, short of a debilitating crunch in the marketplace. The Volcker Fed confronted and defused the huge inflation surge of 1979 but had to confront a sharp economic contraction. Short of that, bubbles have to run their course. Bubbles are functions of unchangeable human nature."

If you agree with the former Chairman, and I do, we will continue to experience bubble after bubble and that we're doomed to repeat this cycle. The solution, in my opinion, for 401(k) plan participants is to measure what's important, for yourself... to accept the fact that conditions change and it is up to you to adapt and change your investment portfolio when it is appropriate. This *is* the End of Buy-and-hold. How will you know when it is appropriate?

We'll cover that in PART SEVEN, Measure What's Important.

xoxoxo

The Map and the Territory

May you live in interesting times.

Having read the book, The Map And the Territory. Risk, Human Nature, and the future of Forecasting by Alan Greenspan, I wanted to share some impressions.

Much of what I've read so far I find disturbing. Greenspan does bring a unique personal perspective to our current economic situation and the elements of Human Nature which brought us here.

Of note are the cascading political decisions which have been made not only during and after the so called Liquidity Crisis; but, well beforehand back to the creation of the Social Security System in 1935 and the Age of Entitlements which he pegs at around the early 1960's.

To frame our National Character immediately before the emergence of the Age of Entitlements he quotes from President Dwight D. Eisenhower's State of the Union Address in 1956 as follows:

"A public office is, indeed, a public trust. None of its aspects is more demanding than the proper management of the public finances. I refer... To the prudent, effective and conscientious use of tax money... over the long-term, a balanced budget is a sure index to thrifty management, in a home, in a business or in the federal government."

This discussion is relevant because savings, government and personal, are the seed capital for future productivity investments which lead to advances in standard of living improvements for the entire society. I'm not going to try to summarize Greenspan's entire book; but, this notion is, I believe, worthy of your consideration.

Savings are critical to your successful retirement. It is there for your *future* day-to- day living, however you imagine it. If it also has the effect of improving the entire society, in my opinion, that's just a bonus.

The other revelation in the book has to do with the inbred human attributes of fear, euphoria and herd behavior. Here we are getting close to what's

133

particularly relevant to you and your 401(k). Greenspan describes herd behavior as being driven by most people's need to achieve the security, emotional and physical, of belonging to a group.

He states it is arguably one of the most important tendencies, second only to fear, and a significant driver of economic activity. He further states herd behavior exaggerates speculation and the business cycle as it distracts us from the facts of markets and draws us to the less relevant views of other people. He goes on to state that herd behavior is a key driver and an essential characteristic of speculative booms and busts.

He seems to have come to the awareness that booms and busts are a function of Human Nature, that Central Banks cannot stop them from happening and this cycle will repeat itself.

And this is where I am going to leave the book for the moment. To reiterate his assertions herd behavior is second only to fear and it distracts us from the facts of markets and draws us to the less relevant views of other people. Does this sound familiar to you?

The title of his book is The Map and the Territory, the thought being the map is NOT the territory. Which reminds me of a quote by Daniel Boone. Asked if he had ever been lost in the wilderness, he thought for a moment and replied, "No, but I was once bewildered for about three days."

We've all been bewildered, I would suggest, because we've been looking at a map. Or, rather... the less relevant views of other people. People promoting their theories, predictions, forecasts and real-time breaking news.

We've been looking at a map and ignoring the territory where we are actually standing. We are bewildered because the territory doesn't match up with the map. In the process we tend to believe the map must be correct and we are just reading it wrong.

Just a quick illustration: I remember doing an overnight hike on the Appalachian Trail. On the hike back out the next day I was following a topographical map while retracing my steps from the previous day. At one point, I realized none of the terrain looked familiar so I stopped. I don't remember how long I stood there studying the map, trying to place myself, looking for the arrow that says "You are Here."

Not finding it, I had a choice, keep trudging forward which would actually have been bush-whacking because there *was* no trail in front of me. Or, I could turn around and go back up the mountain the way I came.

Re-tracing my steps, I came back to the trail. What I realized I had done was miss where the trail veered off to the left. I kept going straight, following what looked like my trail; but, it was actually a track created by downhill water runoff.

I had experienced herd behavior, ignoring the facts. Had I been paying attention, the trail clearly went off to the left.

The point is, regarding your 401(k) investments, you have the tools to view the territory as it actually is. Maps are great. I would never go hiking without one. But, my personal safety depends on trusting what I see on the ground, especially if it doesn't match up with a map.

xoxoxo

There is a Solution

By this point, you should understand I am not a big fan of mass media news, financial or otherwise, because it does nothing to help anyone make sound investment decisions. As for me, I seek out anything which exercises my brain. The hope being I will see something which will help me do something faster/better/easier or save money or cut costs. This curiosity leads me to many subject areas.

I recently came across an article, I'm not sure how to categorize it; but, the idea being discussed was how we cope with the constant onslaught of problems which plague our surroundings. The author suggested, over time, we become desensitized.

That seemed easy enough for me to accept. I clearly remember working as a stock clerk in a hospital pharmacy. The job involved taking a daily inventory of supplies at every nursing station in the morning and refilling them by the end of the day.

What this meant was I moved through-out the hospital, at least twice a day, from the emergency room to the operating room to maternity and Intensive Care and every patient care level in between. I saw some pretty gruesome stuff.

What I found after a period of time was in order to cope with the pain and suffering and yes, even lifeless bodies, was to become desensitized. Now, this was not a conscious act. I didn't decide to become this way. It just happened. I only became aware of it one day walking down a hospital corridor and happened to look into a patient's room. I saw a man who had fallen out of his bed and was calling for help.

I watched myself as I continued past his room. I did not stop to help him and I did not go back to the nursing station to get anyone else to help him. I just continued on my way. I quit that job very soon after because I realized I didn't like who I'd become. I lost my compassion.

Anyway, this memory was triggered while reading the article because the author described the response to hearing all these problems is... we *first* separate ourselves *from* the problem and it makes us less motivated to act or find a solution.

I began thinking, perhaps some of you have become desensitized by financial news. Much of the financial news I see in and out of mainstream media seems to focus on problems. Not solutions. Have we become numb to retirement planning because we've separated ourselves from the problem?

In writing this book, I too have spend time identifying the problems I see, the difference being, I hope, is to communicate solutions.

It has been my hope all along to help you overcome whatever industry shortfalls I've discovered so you *can* have a vibrant future.

So what's the point? I guess the message for today is you *do* have a bright future in front of you. You *can* overcome the pitfalls which are holding you back. If you're angry with each disclosure in the press about how Wall Street is unscrupulous, there is a solution.

If you've had enough, perhaps the best revenge is to reclaim your authority. It's not hard. Remember, smart people seek information in order to do something with it.

Chapter Seven
Measure What's Important

At this point you get to apply all this information to adopt an easy, simple and logical approach to managing your investment portfolio. You will see it does not require a college education. It does not require hundreds of hours of reading reports on mutual funds or exchange traded funds. It does not require keeping up with breaking financial news. It does not require anything more than an understanding of the most basic rules of supply and demand which you already know.

xoxoxo

Point & Figure Charting

By way of introduction, I'm going to walk you through the top five equity mutual funds in most 401(k) plans... using the form of analysis called Point & Figure Charting.

This particular form of investment analysis has been used by Wall Street insiders now for over 130 years. History doesn't tell us when this method first came into existence but it is known that Charles Dow, the Dow of the Dow Jones Industrial Average and Co-Founder of the Wall Street Journal, used this method.

Remember this was a period in history when publicly traded companies were not required to disclose anything about their operations, not even revenue. Charles Dow used this method to create a subscriber newsletter called the Communiqué which was the predecessor of the Wall Street Journal.

Before we begin with the first fund, Let me explain how easy this method is to use. Charles Dow knew the way to understand stock price movement was to look for a trend. The methodology, as it was used by Mr. Dow, was constructed with a simple graph as seen here.

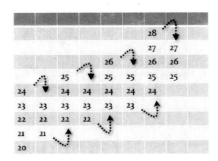

The numbers represent prices. In the first column, prices are rising from 20 to 24. Shifting one column to the right, the prices are falling from 23 to 21. Shifting again, one column to the right, prices are again rising from 22 to 25. Columns switch from prices either rising or falling. I'll explain in a bit the rule when to switch columns.

Clearly, this chart is somewhat hard on the eyes; however, over time, for easier reading, the prices inside the chart were replaced by "X"s and "O"s.

"X"s represented prices rising and "O"s represented prices falling. That's it ! Now, on the far left column, we have numbers which represent a range of prices and the "X"s and "O"s represent times when the stock achieved that price. In the case of the chart below, the price fell from 23 to 20 represented by each "O" in each box. (Remember, "O"s only appear when prices are falling.)

Then, once there is enough demand to raise the price at least three boxes, we shift one column to the right and continue with the chart. The price rose from 21 to 24, in this case four boxes, so we shift one column to the right and add four ""X"s. Continuing along we note selling was once again strong enough to drive the price back down to 20, in this case four boxes, so, we shift one column to the right and enter four "O"s. After a time, we note demand was once again strong enough to raise the price at least three boxes. Again, we shift one column to the right and enter four "X"s to 24. But this time demand or buying continues to drive the price up to 25 so we add an "X" in each box up to 25.

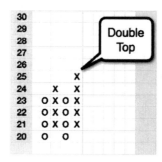

Of note, the "X" at 25 is called a "Double Top" because there was sufficient demand to exceed the previous top of 24. This is one of the two fundamental building blocks of the Point & Figure Method.

The other fundamental building block of the Point & Figure Method is the "Double Bottom" shown below. Remember "X"s represent prices rising and "O"s represent prices falling. That's it !

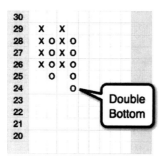

In the case of the "Double Bottom" supply is strong enough for the price to go below the previous bottom, in this case at 25.

The rule for switching columns is called the "Three Box Reversal Method." In other words, there must be "significant" evidence of supply or demand to move from column to column. Why? Because the beauty of the "Three Box Reversal Method" is to take the noise out of daily price movement. The charts which result only show significant price movement.

A Point & Figure Chart is just a graphic representation of the struggle between supply, prices falling, and demand, prices rising. Everything there is to know about an investment is incorporated in the price because price is the place where buyers and sellers agree on a value and a transaction takes place. It represents real buyers and real sellers voting with real dollars.

American Funds Growth Fund of America

The easiest way to explain this method is to walk you through a few charts. Let's begin with American Funds Growth Fund of America to show you how you can analyze it yourself. The ticker symbol that we're going to use as a proxy for American funds growth fund of America is AGTHX.

There are a number of websites where you can get charts. Www.stockcharts.com is free and it's fairly easy to navigate. These are the instructions to pull up a chart. If you know the ticker symbol for a fund offered in your plan you can use these instructions to see that fund. So here we go...

Once you're on the Landing page you'll see a baby blue box titled "welcome to stock charts.com." Just above that you'll see a Blue grey banner that covers the width of the page. Inside the banner you'll see the text "create a chart", a drop-down menu with the default set at "sharp chart', a box which says "enter company name or symbol", and a button that says "go."

Click on the drop-down menu. The next type of chart is P and F chart. Click on that; and, then in the box which says "enter company name or symbol" go ahead and enter the symbol of American Funds Growth Fund of America which is AGTHX. Click on the "go" button.

This is what you should see...

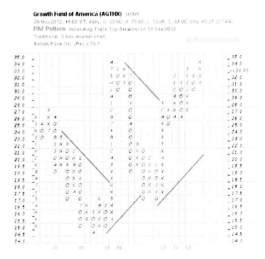

(Chart courtesy of StockCharts.com)

Down the left column and the right column, you'll see numbers from 35.0 to 14.0. These numbers represent prices. Across the bottom of the graph you'll see numbers 01, 02, 03, 08, 10, 11 and 12. These numbers represent years. Inside the chart you'll see columns that are filled with either "Xs" which are prices going up or "Os" which are prices going down. In some of the boxes you will see numbers one through nine or capital letters A, B, or C. The numbers one through nine represent the months January through September and A, B and C represent the months October, November and December.

The first thing we want to do is expand the chart so we can get more detailed information. Just below the chart you'll see a line with the following blue links: instructions, understanding, print, about P&F alerts, about price objectives, and Past data. Just below that line you see a box titled "chart attributes" which is were we are going to focus first.

Look for the drop-down menu to the far right for "chart size." Click on the drop-down box and find the size identified as mega and in parentheses 1000. Click on that. In the next large box titled "chart scale" click on the drop-down box for scaling method, and select "user defined." Right next to the "scaling method" drop down box you will see where you can change the "box size." The default is set at "one." Change that value to 0.5. Skip down below the box titled "duration" and the box titled "chart overlays" to the button that says "update chart." Click on 'update chart" now.

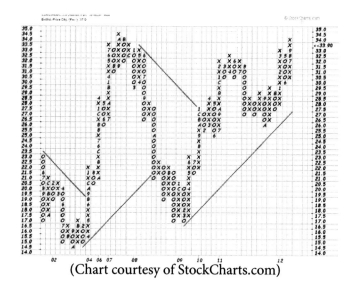

(Chart courtesy of StockCharts.com)

The first thing you should know about point & figure charts is they do not measure time; they measure price movement. It's a graphical representation of the battle between supply and demand.

The most powerful thing about point and figure charting is it measures what is. It has nothing to do with predicting, it's all about measuring. It measures historical prices to determine whether supply or demand is in control of today's price movement.

You can't fake supply and demand using this method because we are capturing the activity of real people using real money voting with their wallets.

Prices are rising or prices are falling. The only reason prices rise is because there are more buyers willing to buy then there are sellers willing to sell. The only reason prices fall is because there are more sellers willing to sell then there are buyers willing to buy. Any other reason given for the price movement is simply a story. Why?

Because what would the media have to fill the space in the business news if they said "The stock market fell 350 points today because there were more sellers than buyers." The media is in the business of selling advertising. That's how they make money. The more viewers they have the more they can charge for advertising. The way they get more viewers is to manufacture drama. All drama is conflict. Create the most dramatic story with conflict - in other words, find someone to blame - and you will get viewers.

How realistic is it to believe some expert can pin a single reason (or even 2 or 3) for the market movement in a day? Looking at just the New York Stock Exchange:

In 1961 the average trading volume on the New York Stock Exchange reached 4 million shares per day.

20 years later in 1982, the New York Stock Exchange trading volume reached 100 million shares exchanged in one day.

In 1992, the average daily volume on the New York Stock Exchange exceeded 200 million shares.

In 1997, October 27, the volume on the exchange reached 1 billion shares for the first time.

In 2005, on June 24, the New York Stock Exchange had it single largest volume trading day when over 3 billion shares changed hands.

By, 2009 the volume crossed over the 7 billion share mark and today is between 3 and 4 billion shares… per day!

So these commentators have a crystal ball and can read the minds of buyers and sellers of billions of shares every day? Right.

But I digress. Getting back to the Growth Fund of America chart, focus on the high point which is easy to find on the graph. Look to the top of the chart. See the "X" in the box above the capital letter "A" along the axis corresponding to the price of 34.5? Got it? Great.

Reading the Chart, we can tell the price reached that level in the month of October. Remember? A = October; B = November; and, C = December. Now, look down the same column on the graph and you will notice at the bottom of the scale going across the column is between the '07 and '08. So, we know the 34.5 price occurred during October 2007.

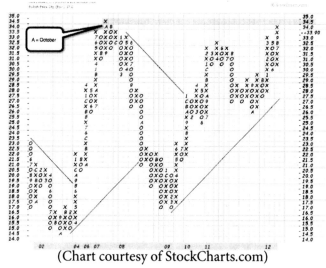

(Chart courtesy of StockCharts.com)

Following along, shifting one column to the right there is a B followed by 4 "Os." What that's telling us is the price of American Funds Growth Fund of America's shares dropped in the month November to $32 per share. Shifting over one more column to the right we see that in December, designated by the letter "C' followed by two "Xs" above it, the price of Growth Fund of America shares rose to 33.5.

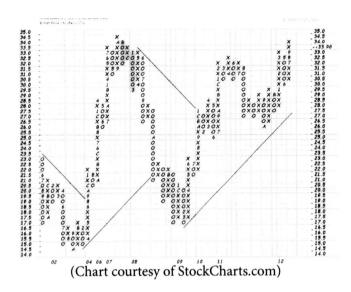

(Chart courtesy of StockCharts.com)

Now it begins to get interesting. Shifting over one more column to the right, beginning with the number one in the column followed by 6 zeros and the number three, we see that a significant change occurred in the beginning of 2008.

Remember we said prices fall when there are more sellers willing to sell then there are buyers willing to buy. Notice that from 2002 through 2007 every time supply took control (prices falling) of the American Funds Growth Fund of America shares, demand came back and the price exceeded the last highest price.

In November 2003 the price got to $17 per share; then in February 2003 the prices fell to $15 a share; thereafter, prices rose through 2005 up to $22 a share before a brief retreat to 20.5 in August 2004. In September 2005 through April 2006 the price steadily rose to 28.5. During May and June 2006 the price retreated to $26 per share. And then from July 2006 through July 2007 the price rose to 33.5. August 2007 saw a brief retreat to $31 a share followed by the rise to its all-time high of 34.5 by October of that year.

To recap the highs were $17 a share $22, $28.5, $33.5 and $34.5. Each time there was a price pullback the new low was higher than the old low - right up until we get to 2008.

In 2008 not only did we not have enough demand to make a new high (higher than 34.5) but we experienced enough supply for prices to fall below the previous low of 32 and the previous low of 31. By March the new low was 29.5.

For a point and figure Chartist, what this tells us is, the shares gave not one, but two technical "sell signals." Just a side note, a technical "Sell Signal" is industry jargon. It does not mean to run out and sell your position.

What it does tell us is that supply has now taken control of the position. As we watch for further development we noticed in April and May 2008 the price actually does go up from 29.5 to 33. However in June the share price reverses down before it could make a new high which would have occurred at 34. This confirms that supply has taken control of the position and prices will likely fall.

Does this mean that the Growth Fund of America fund managers were doing a poor job? Absolutely not! They were following their mandate to invest in companies that appeared, in the opinion of the portfolio managers, to offer superior opportunities for growth of capital. The one thing portfolio managers cannot control, regardless of how good they are, is the general direction of the market which will weigh heavily on any equity mutual fund.

Unfortunately for you, even if portfolio managers did recognize a market moving against them and the negative impact on the portfolio, they are powerless to get out of the way. Why?

Because by mandate, within the operating policies established for the fund at the time, they were limited in the amount of cash they were allowed to hold in the portfolio. They believed if you wanted more cash in your overall portfolio, you and you alone would liquidate their shares to raise whatever level of cash you desired as a defensive strategy.

What could you have done? The prudent thing to do would have been to have waited to see if the last low was exceeded. Which in this case, would've been at 29. At that point it would've become perfectly clear supply was in control and prices would likely fall. You could have avoided the decline in price all the way back to 17 where it was in November 2003.

Remember point and figure charts do not have anything to do with predicting. It's all about measuring.

Ok. That's as far as we are going to go with the Growth Fund of America as a training tool. Europe Pacific Growth Fund will be up next. Just a side note. Even if we are not using one of the funds offered in your 401(k) plan, you can still benefit by following along. The principals we discuss apply to all of them.

Euro Pacific Growth Fund

Simply to restate: the goal here is to help you understand how to look at your 401(k) investment options in a logical, organized systematic way by reviewing the top five mutual funds offered in 401(k) plans today. The next mutual fund is Euro Pacific Growth Fund, which is also another American Funds offering.

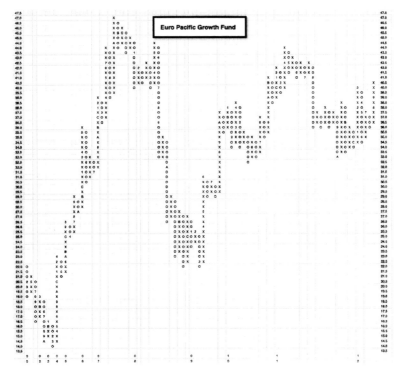

Remember the objective here is to help you break down barriers to making better 401(k) investment choices. We will do this by helping you understand an investment method that has been used by Wall Street insiders now for over 130 years.

This method is called point and figure charting. We use this method because of all the forms of technical analysis; this is, in my opinion, the most easily understood yet accurate method of investment analysis. If you can count to three, you can create and understand a point and figure chart. A 10-year-old can read one of these charts.

They are simply a way to determine if supply or demand is in control. Once you can see this, the frustration of riding markets up only to ride them back down can be eliminated. And, decision making becomes much easier because there are clear trends which can be seen as well as price support and resistance levels

Just a side note, when I originally prepared this presentation for the YouTube Channel, someone suggested I read the www.stockcharts.com terms of service. If I understand the terms of service correctly, users are free to link to the website but not to specific charts. I sent a message to the company to ask if the last episode on YouTube was a violation of the terms of service.

While waiting for their response, I used charts derived from a paid, institutional level service which I have been using for over a decade. The standard required disclosure is probably appropriate at this point - past performance is not indicative of future results.

Remember, this is not about predicting, it's about measuring. I was first introduced to this method over 30 years ago and I can assure you this is an art, not a science; however, it is remarkable how trends are easily identified and patterns repeat themselves regardless of the investment being analyzed.

Take a quick look at Euro Pacific Growth Fund and notice that the price movement for Euro Pacific Growth Fund is very similar to what we saw in the Growth Fund of America from 2002 through 2008.

From 2002 through 2007 each of the funds demonstrated a series of higher highs and higher lows. A clear visual uptrend until we get to supply winning the battle in the beginning 2008 through 2009 with each of the funds demonstrating a series of lower lows and lower highs.

Let me direct your attention on the column of "0"s in between the years 09 and 10. The last "0" in the column preceded by the number three is in the box for the value of $22 a share. Reading the chart we know that this value occurred in March 2009.

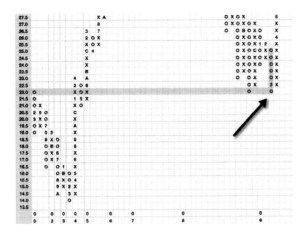

The method being used for chart construction here is called the three box reversal method. Which simply means the only time we switch columns is if there is a significant change in price.

This is how it works. At the end of each trading day we simply look at the closing price (in the case of a mutual fund); and, if we are in a column of "0"s the first question to ask is:

"Did the price fall to the value in the next box down or lower?"

If it has, we simply place an "O" in the next box and we are done for that trading day. (Actually, place an "O" in as many boxes down as the values dictate.)

If the price has not fallen to the value in the next box down, the next question to ask is:

"Did the price rise to the value (at least) three boxes above the last entry?"

Hence the three box reversal method. If it did not, we make no entry on the chart and we are done for the trading day.

Take a look at March 2009 where the last entry in the column of "O"s is at the price value of $22 a share. Just to illustrate the three box reversal process, if the price had fallen to the 21.50 mark, we would have continued adding "O"s into the column. However, since the price rose to at least 23.50 per-share we moved one column to the right and started adding "Xs" which are prices going up.

So we are now in a column of "X"s … in that column we see the numbers four, five and six which tells us that the prices continue to rise, without a three box reversal, throughout April May and June.

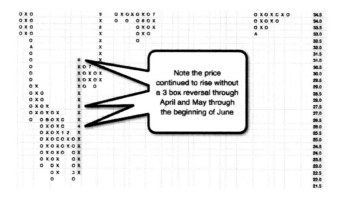

Between June and July there <u>was</u> a three box reversal. In fact, in this case, the price fell four boxes so we did shift to another column from "X"s to "O"s - which represent prices falling.

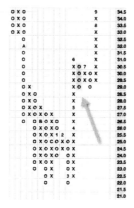

In July we saw a three box reversal <u>up</u> so we move to a column of "X"s - followed by another three box reversal (<u>down</u>) shifting to a column of "0"s – and, another three box reversal (<u>up</u>) shifting to a column of "X"s.

By August, represented by the number 8, the price rose to 33.50; and, by October, the price rose to 36.50.

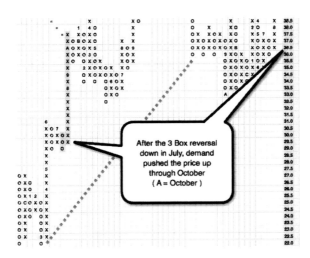

Can you see by using the three box reversal method, we take the noise out of the typical chart which captures every price however insignificant it may be?

In October 2009, the price reaches a high of 37.50 before the three box reversal down to 36 and then one more box down to 35.50. By January 2010 the price reverses up to a high of 38 which is the first technical "Buy Signal." It's called a technical "Buy Signal" because it exceeded the previous high of 37.50. It is not a call to action. It is just industry jargon used by the P&F chartist.

Some significant observations on the period that we just covered, notice that in June we had the three box reversal (down) to 29 followed by a three box reversal up in July and the three box reversal down again; but, the price stopped at 29. It did not make a new low.

So it is said 29 is an area of support because at that price demand reappears and prices begin to rise once again. The significance of the price rise to 37.5 is - it crossed what is referred to as the "down trend" line. On the chart, it is a 45 degree line represented by the blue dots originating at the top of the decline from 44.50 in May 2008.

On this chart, the "up trend" line is established in March 2009, just below the price of 22 where Euro Pacific Growth ultimately found support. This is the 45 degree line represented by the red dots which held until August of 2011.

In all the years I've worked with P&F Charts, these trend lines remain strong areas of price resistance and support. In other words, violation of the trend line is a significant event and merits our attention.

Ok. That's as far as we are going to go with the Euro Pacific Growth Fund as a training example. Next we will be using Davis New York Venture Fund. Just a reminder, even if we are not using one of the funds offered in your 401(k) plan, you can still benefit by following along. The principals we discuss apply to all of them.

xoxoxo

Davis New York Venture Fund

The next mutual fund is Davis NY Venture Fund and the ticker symbol is a NYVTX:

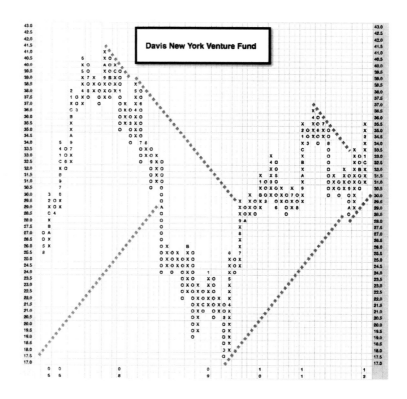

Before we begin with January 2010, take a quick look at the chart and notice that the price movement for Davis NY Venture Fund is very similar to what we saw in the Growth Fund of America and EuroPacific growth fund. From 2003 through 2007 each of the funds demonstrated a series of higher highs and higher lows. A clear visual uptrend until we get to supply winning the battle in the beginning 2008 through 2009 with each of the funds demonstrating a series of lower lows and lower highs.

You will see the same pattern demonstrated in the rest of the funds to follow.

151

Quick review, down the left and right column, you'll see numbers from 43 to 17.0. These numbers represent prices. Across the bottom of the graph you'll see numbers 02, through 12. These numbers represent years. Inside the chart you'll see columns that are filled with either "Xs" which are prices going up or "Os" which are prices going down. In some of the boxes you will see numbers one through nine or capital letters A, B, or C. The numbers one through nine represent the months January through September and A, B and C represent the months October, November and December.

Focus your attention on the column of "X"s in between the years 10 and 11. The last "X" in the column preceded by the number four is in the box for the value of $33 a share. By this point you should be able to tell this value occurred in April 2010.

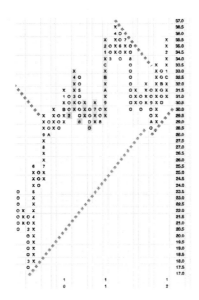

The numbers which appear inside the boxes as well as the capital letters A, B and C are for reference only. Remember, these charts measure price movement. They do not measure time. The purpose of the charts are to aid in the visualization of supply and demand as represented by actual transactions at a particular price.

Continuing to read this chart, we notice there was a 3 box reversal down in May and price continued to fall until June. Notice the price corresponding to the box with the number "6" inside, was at 29. Notice too, this was a technical "sell signal" because the price was lower than the last low on the chart at $29.5 per share.

152

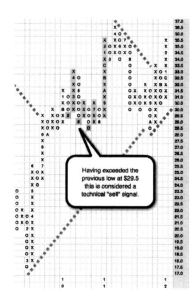

A technical "sell signal" is not a call to action. It is simply a term of art used by the P&F chartist because any investment being measured can only be on a technical "buy signal" or a technical "sell signal." There is no middle ground. We will cover the importance of this distinction later.

Also in the June timeframe, we see demand overpower the price and a 3 box reversal up; but, the price, demand, stops at $30.5 before another 3 box reversal down. However, there is sufficient supply to push the price to another new low at 28.5.

At that price, demand reenters the market, and buyers drive the price all the way back up to $30.5; however, it stops there when supply reenters in August and sellers drive the price back down to $29. Can you see the constant battle between supply and demand, sellers and buyers - sometime quickly, sometimes slowly? If you are actively measuring, you will see this clearly.

If we follow the action just a little further, at the price of 29, buyers reenter, there is sufficient demand for a 3 box reversal up in September; and, demand remains in control through February 2011. This is clear because throughout that timeframe supply never enters with enough force to achieve a 3 box reversal down until March.

The 3 box reversal method only captures significant price movement; and, that's all we want to observe.

It is worth repeating - past performance is not indicative of future results. Charting is about measuring, not predicting. I mentioned before, having used this for decades, I can assure you this is an art, not a science. What occurred in September is a testament to that fact. Let me explain. Having given two, consecutive technical "sell signals" a P&F chartist would assume the price would continue down for <u>no other reason than statistical probability says it should</u>. But, clearly, it did not. Which is why we measure. We may <u>anticipate</u> price movement; but, we do not predict it. If and when conditions change we change.

Predicting comes with an emotional attachment of being right or wrong. I have seen "experts" make predictions for over thirty years now and invariably, when they are wrong, there is a defensive attitude which creeps into their voice and they begin to justify why some force ruined their perfectly good prediction. If only this or that did or didn't happen they would have been right!

Small consolation for the investor who placed their money on an "expert" opinion ruined by unforeseen forces.

In the world of investments, it's OK to BE wrong. STAYING wrong is what gets expensive.

Ok. That's as far as we are going to go with Davis NY Venture Fund today. Next we will be using Fidelity Contrafund.

If you want to grab the earliest publication on point and figure charting, it was released to the public in 1933 by Victor DeVilliers and Owen Taylor. They described it as the only method of anticipating stock price movements based on logical and scientific mechanical principals. You can still grab a copy on Amazon.

xoxoxo

Fidelity Contrafund

Imagine you are Charles Henry Dow in the late 1800s. Stock prices are easily manipulated by rumor and financial news reporters have been bribed with stock tips or free stock to spin positive stories so as to pump stock prices. Publicly traded companies are not required to disclose any financial information to the general public and won't be until 1933 and 1934.

Just as Charles Dow discovered, what we are showing you is a logical, organized, systematic way to measure supply and demand. No predicting. No

154

forecasting. No more media driven frenzy punching your emotional hot-buttons.

All we are highlighting is an investment method used by Wall Street insiders now for over 130 years. It's called point and figure charting. If you Google the term point and figure charting, you will likely see Dorsey Wright & Associates. Tom Dorsey has authored a number of books on the subject; and, I consider him a friend and mentor. I first met Tom when we both worked in a regional investment banking firm in the early eighties.

To continue... next we are going to review Fidelity Contrafund. The ticker symbol is FCNTX:

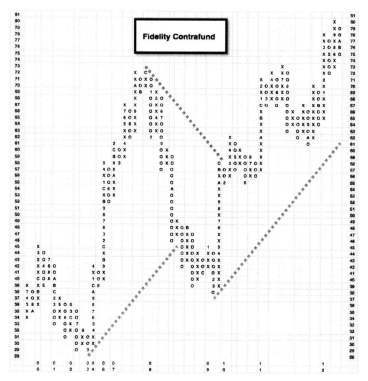

Again, take a quick look at the chart and notice that the price movement for Fidelity Contrafund is very similar to what we saw in the Growth Fund of America, EuroPacific Growth Fund and Davis NY Venture Fund. From 2003 through 2007 each of the funds demonstrated a series of higher highs and higher lows. A clear visual uptrend until we get to supply winning the battle in the beginning of 2008 through 2009 with each of the funds demonstrating a series of lower lows and lower highs.

You will see the same pattern demonstrated in the last fund and I'll explain at that time why this occurred.

Ok. Let's focus on Fidelity Contrafund. You'll notice one difference in this chart vs. the last three we've used. Previously, we formatted the charts using a value of $0.50 per box so we could see the price movement more clearly. Here we adjusted the box size to $1.00 per box to **slow** the chart down. Again, so we can see the price movement more clearly. At $0.50 per box the price is simply too fast which doesn't serve our purpose.

Why? Because we're NOT interested in using this method to jump in and out of investments. We simply want to identify the trend as well as <u>significant</u> price levels of support and resistance in order to manage the investment risk.

Ok. We took Davis NY Venture Fund through January 2011. So, let's continue there. By February, the chart hit a price of $71 followed by a 3 box reversal **down** in March. The price continued down one more box to $67 before it completed a 3 box reversal **up** in April. Demand continued to drive the price up two more boxes to a new high of $72.

By June, supply reenters with sufficient force to complete a 3 box reversal **down** and continues to push the price back to $67 where it find support at the immediate past low. At $67, demand takes hold again in July, completes a 3 box reversal **up** and continues to drive the price past the last high of $72 and stops at $73 which is now a "triple top buy signal." because this high exceeded the last three highs.

Now it gets interesting because when supply returns in August, it's with such power that it completes a 3 box reversal **down** and continues to drive the price through the near-term support at $67 and continues on to a low of $63. The move below support, when the price hit $66, was a technical "sell signal."

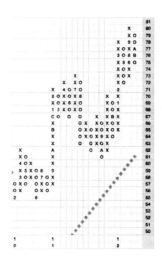

There is a maxim among Point & Figure Chartists that the **first** "sell signal" in an uptrend is typically false. That proved to be the case in June 2010. However, we are about to have a **second** "sell signal" in an uptrend: and, it's worthy of our attention.

There is a brief 3 box reversal **up** followed by a 3 box reversal **down** which follows through to a new low at $62 which is a "double bottom sell signal" because this low exceeded the last two lows. This move confirms supply is in control.

Yet, there is another push of demand which completes a 3 box reversal **up** and the price continues up to a price of $67 which is another "Buy Signal." All this action takes place in the month of August. In September, Supply takes back control and completes a 3 box reversal **down** and by October we see the price move to $61 which is a "triple bottom sell signal."

Can you see the constant battle between supply and demand and that, at any given point, the chart is either on a buy signal or a sell signal? There is nothing arbitrary about that designation. It is either on a buy signal or a sell signal. There is no middle ground. There is nothing subjective about it. Everyone who understands point and figure charting will agree because the laws of supply and demand are irrefutable. This is why the method is historically referred to as "Scientific" because **anyone** observing the same data will come up with the same conclusion.

This is not the case with fundamental analysis because given the same company being analyzed research analysts rarely agree on the merits of a particular investment. Why? Because they each make their own **independent,** assumptions about the **future** prospects of the investment in question. I won't even go into the buy side bias of all fundamental research analysis and the ridiculously low number of sell recommendations on the street.

The only bias that can enter into this form of investment analysis is human nature; and, it does in a number of forms. Think of it as reading instruments in an airplane. There are occasions when a pilot sees the instrument readings but believes they must be wrong.

In this case, it is not so much a belief as it is a hope. I have seen a number of investors fall back on the idea that "it's different this time" and refuse to believe their own eyes.

I've done it. And, I believe anyone who's ever invested in the market has too.

The good news is that the chart will guide you; and, hopefully you will not stay wrong for very long.

Another form of this bias is forming a preconceived idea about an investment. In other words, an investor may say "I got burned in international stocks or in the dot com bubble and I'll never do that again."

This kind of thinking is, I believe, more common among investors who do not practice some form of technical analysis, like Point & Figure Charting. They are limited by their emotions because they do not have a barometer which is indifferent to opinion anymore than your outdoor temperature gauge. The weather **forecast** may be for a high of 75 degrees; but if the temperature gauge outside your door says 50 degrees, you'll dress accordingly.

The point is, charts will tell you what is. It is up to you to determine what you will do with the data.

All of this reminds me what my father told me many years ago. When asked what the stock market will do, J.P Morgan (banker, financier, businessman) replied:

"It will fluctuate."

It is worth repeating - past performance is not indicative of future results. Charting is about measuring, not predicting. I mentioned before, having used this for decades, I can assure you this is an art, not a science. Which is why we measure. We may <u>anticipate</u> price movement; but, we do not predict it. If and when conditions change we change.

Remember, in the world of investments, it's OK to BE wrong. STAYING wrong is what gets expensive.

Ok. That's as far as we are going to go with Fidelity Contrafund. Next we will cover the Vanguard 500 Index Fund.

xoxoxo

Vanguard 500 Index Fund

I remember when I first saw this method in the early 1980s. It was before Microsoft's IPO and before I got my hands on a desktop computer: the Apple IIe. Once I understood it I was surprised and a little angry. My educational training and career had been founded in detailed financial analysis; and, the idea that something as simple as charting supply and demand to anticipate stock price just didn't sit well. At the time, I was doing financial analysis using 14 column PAPER spreadsheets and a mechanical pencil.

If it was this easy, why didn't everyone use it?

I came to believe the why wasn't important. I started charting by hand, myself and thousands of charts later, I let go of "news" and "research" and "expert opinion." It was liberating.

Accepting what is and focusing on the truth with a logical, organized, systematic way to measure stock price movement works for me. No predicting. No forecasting. No media driven frenzy.

So far, we've used four of the top five mutual funds found in 401(k) plans today to highlight how the method works. The last fund to review is the Vanguard 500 Index Fund. The ticker symbol is: VFINX

Before we get started, take a moment to look over all the charts we've presented so far. No doubt, you've noticed from 2003 through 2007 each of the funds demonstrated a series of higher highs and higher lows. A clear visual uptrend until we get to supply winning the battle in the beginning 2008 through 2009 with each of the funds demonstrating a series of lower lows and lower highs.

I promised I'd explain why this occurred. Buried deep in each prospectus you will discover a common disclosure item. It speaks to a restriction on the percentage of cash the mutual fund will be allowed to hold in the overall portfolio. The maximum being along the order of 10%.

I don't know when or why this restriction came into play. I suspect it was born of some government regulation. The intent, I believe, was to protect investors from being overcharged. Let me explain: equity portfolio management fees typically range from 0.75% to 1.50%. Management fees for money market accounts typically run 15 100ths of one percent. (0.15%)

Someone must have believed investors, on their own, were able to consciously determine how much cash was appropriate; and, would get there by selling fund shares themselves. This is the disconnect between Mutual Funds implying they will do it all for you and the attitude that individual funds are but a tool to satisfy an asset allocation strategy. In other words, the Mutual Funds are not responsible.

The unintended consequence was, in the wake of the so called liquidity crisis in 2008, even if mutual fund portfolio managers wanted to avoid the freight train barreling down the tracks at 90mph they were tied to the train tracks... and so were you, if you thought fund managers would do this for you.

This is where the value of Point & Figure Charting comes to the aid of investors.

Clearly, SOMEONE should be watching the big picture. If fund managers are not watching the big picture. If your broker is not watching the big picture. And, if your employer is not watching the big picture. You owe it to yourself and your family to pick up these simple tools or find someone who will do it for you. This is simple. You deserve to know how to protect your money.

Ok. Let's get back to the Vanguard 500 Index Fund.

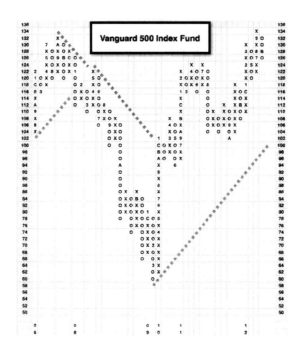

You'll notice, just as we did for Fidelity Contrafund, we adjusted the box size for the Vanguard 500 index Fund. In this case we are using a box size equal to $2.00 per share. We've done this for no other reason than to **slow** the chart down so we can see more clearly the <u>significant</u> price movement. Again, we are not interested in using this method to jump in and out of investments. We are looking for a way to manage investment risk. The way we do this is to identify levels of support and resistance and the overall trend in the price movement.

To Quote Bernard Baruch, noted financier & economist who lived from 1870 to 1965:
"Don't try to buy at the bottom and sell at the top. It can't be done except by liars."

Ok. We took Fidelity Contrafund through September 2011. So, let's continue there.

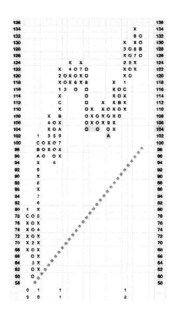

By October, the chart broke through support at $104 and stopped at $102. Shifting one column to the right because of the 3 box reversal to 108. Note we are using a value of 2 points per box so the price has to move 6 points to complete a 3 box reversal. Demand continues to drive the price 5 more boxes to 118. When the price reached 114, it was a new buy signal because the violation of support at 104 was a sell signal. Sometimes buy and sell signals come quickly and it is up to the investor to exercise personal judgement.

One of the ways to do this is to set up <u>mental</u> "stop loss" targets. I am not an advocate of automatic stop losses. I prefer to have a choice. A stop loss is another risk management tool. The question to ask yourself is "how much of a loss am I willing to take?" Successful investors always manage the downside risk because they know the key to wealth accumulation rests upon the avoidance of catastrophic losses.

Again, this depends on where you bought the position. If you bought at 60 the move to 102 may not bother you. You may give it more time to see if it violates the last support at 94 and make a decision from there. Yet, if you bought at 104 in March of 2010 you may want to sell some or all of the position at 102. It's a choice. It's always a choice if you are measuring price movement. If you are simply doing buy and hope you would have no choice because you wouldn't know <u>what</u> to do.

Make sense?

If you've been following the last four charts carefully, you can easily read the chart from October 2011 through October 2012. Despite the fact that 12 months have passed the chart has only added 5 columns. All we see are higher lows and higher highs. It's a very orderly uptrend even though we've had:

1. Tsunami in Japan.
2. Moammar Gadhafi ousted, killed.
3. Steve Jobs dies.
4. Presidential election in the US and abroad.
5. Spain accepts a 100 Billion Euro Bailout deal.
6. Greece still fighting austerity plans.
7. Facebook IPO.
8. Moody's downgrades 15 major banks in the UK, US, Canada and Europe.
9. Osama bin Laden killed.
10. Hurricane Sandy hits the Northeast US and closed the NYSE for 2 days. And,
11. The press is now promoting the worry of the "fiscal cliff".

Can you see how news is not important to price movement; it's the markets response to news, if any, which is important. Judging from the last twelve month on this chart the market has been indifferent to the news. Nothing major has happened.

How much time have you spent in the last twelve months consuming financial news? Did it make any difference? Could you have been doing anything more productive or enjoyable with your time?

If you had been measuring market prices using the Point & Figure methodology, think of all the time and anxiety you could have saved.

Oh by the way, because the media is in the business of publishing content 24/7; and, ALL of it is sold with drama and importance, isn't it like the boy who cried wolf? If ALL of it is important - none of it is more important than any of it to help you make better 401(k) investment choices. Food for thought. Turn off the media and start measuring.

xoxoxo

NYSE Bullish Percent Index

So far we've considered the top five mutual funds found in 401(k) plans in light of a user-friendly investment method which has been developed over 130 years.

The takeaway being none are particularly unique. American Funds Growth
Fund of America and Euro Pacific Growth Fund, the Davis NY Venture Fund,
Fidelity Contrafund and Vanguard 500 Index Fund all share one thing in
common. They all crashed in the Liquidity Crisis in 2008.

Ok. Let's assume the investment choices you have in your 401(k) are different
from the top five funds we've looked at so far. It shouldn't take very much time
to pull up a typical price/volume chart on any financial website and look at how
they behaved in 2008. I would venture to guess they all crashed. No surprise
there.

In all likelihood, they also crashed in the Dot.com Bubble and the Crash of
1987.

Let's talk about process.

A common theme among money managers is what we call a "top down"
investment approach. In simple terms all that means is beginning the
investment process with a view of the overall market first. Are we in a bull
market or a bear market?

Investment professionals know that just like boats in a marina when the tide is
rising all boats will go up; and, when the tide is falling all boats will go down.
The market is much the same.

So we need a process to tell us, objectively, where we are in any given market
cycle.

Clearly the financial media is of no help. And, as for me, I'll agree with George
Bernard Shaw's statement "If all the economists were laid end to end, they'd
never reach a conclusion."

Fortunately, there've been some brilliant minds who came before us. Most
notably a gentleman by the name of Abraham W. Cohen, commonly referred
to as "AW." He was a graduate of Harvard Law, who authored a book in 1947
titled "Stock Market Timing." He then founded Chartcraft Weekly Service and
became the publication's first editor.

Chartcraft is still around. You can find them at investors intelligence dot com.

AW Cohen expanded on the thinking of another analyst by the name of Ernest
J. Staby who published "Stock Market Trading; point and figure investing made

easy" in 1947 which was re-released in 1949 under the title "The Chartcraft method of point and figure trading: a scientific approach to the mechanics of stock market trading."

Staby realized that charts in general were poor tools for identifying market tops and bottoms because at market tops, most charts look great and at market bottoms most charts look terrible.

He was looking to fashion an indicator which would be bearish at market tops and bullish at market bottoms.

The idea being such an indicator would help investors become less aggressive as the market approached high risk levels and more comfortable in taking positions when the market was washed out and the risk was in fact relatively low.

In 1955, A. W. Cohen introduced the New York Stock Exchange Bullish Percent Index.

Recall the previous mention of the term, the technical "Buy Signal" ?

This is why the term is important. The New York Stock Exchange Bullish Percent Index is a percentage of stocks, traded on the NYSE, which are on a Point & Figure Buy Signal. Remember, any stock can either be on a buy signal or a sell signal. There is no middle ground, no grey area.

So, tallying the number of stocks on a buy signal and dividing by the number of stock in the sample (the NYSE in this case) we can create a scale from 0 to 100% to objectively measure the market temperature, so to speak.

If 70% of stocks on the NYSE are on a buy signal your risk is greater than if only 10, 20 or 30% of stocks are on a buy signal.

It's a supply and demand issue. If 70% of stocks are on a buy signal, it means that most everyone who wants to be in the market is already invested. This becomes evident when a stock broker calls a client to buy something and the client says, "great idea, what should we sell?"

At the other end of the spectrum, if the NYSE Bullish Percent Index has fallen below the 30% threshold, and is marching north once again, it means most everyone who wanted to sell has already sold. They're done; but, some buyers are cautiously, quietly beginning to reenter the market.

However, this is not obvious to the public because it is not obvious to the financial media. By the time it becomes obvious to the public and the financial media, the NYSE Bullish Percent is already on the approach to 70%.

Supply and demand, fear and greed are the forces in the market which move price both generally and specifically. This has always been the case and as long as human beings are human, it will always be the case.

To quote Jesse Livermore, probably one of the most flamboyant characters Wall Street has ever seen, "Wall Street never changes, the pockets change, the suckers change, the stocks change, but Wall Street never changes, because human nature never changes."

What I have observed over the years is the financial media never gets this right. When the market is overheated, in other words when the NYSE Bullish Percent is 70% plus, the media cannot help but cheer because they can never see the end in sight. When the NYSE Bullish Percent has moved below 30% and has already begun to rise again, the financial media can only report gloom and doom.

What's the point? Why is this relevant? What does this have to do with my 401(k)?

Choices. Better choices. I believe the secret to wealth accumulation is avoiding catastrophic losses. Cruse control is a nice feature for a long drive; but, you wouldn't consider taking even a short nap while driving at 65 miles per hour.

Traffic conditions change, road conditions change, the weather changes and light conditions change. And, guess what... so does the market.

So what choices do you have the next time market supply takes control? You can manually change speed; stop automatic investment of your regular contributions; reallocate some of your portfolio to cash; or, you may dial down the most aggressive asset class investments you have. They're just choices.

The fact is without taking a little time to measure what's happening in the market, you will have no choices because you won't know what to do. In turn, you'll continue to get whipsawed by the market.

xoxoxo

Bullish Percent Concept

Having introduced the NYSE Bullish Percent, it would be irresponsible to have you think this is the only market gauge you need. Yet, that is what I was taught early in my apprenticeship. The reason being, it didn't change very often.

However, over my career, I've become less and less confident in relying on just this one indicator.

Perhaps it began to move more frequently than had been observed since the mid-1950s because of the adoption of personal computers, the internet and raw data flowing without restriction.

Remember, what we are measuring here is the percent of stocks on the New York Stock Exchange which are on a Point & Figure "Buy" signal. We do this because the overall demand for stocks (or lack of demand) will have an influence on all individual stocks. It's the all boats in a marina analogy… when the tide is rising, all boats will rise. When the tide is falling, all boats will fall.

In turn, when demand for stocks is rising, all stocks will rise. When demand is falling, all stocks will fall, in general. The same is true for the mutual fund investments in your 401(k). So it makes sense to watch a broad universe of stocks, not just a popular index.

To put this in perspective for today, I view this indicator not as an On-Off switch. I, personally, view it as more of a dimmer switch. In 2013, I did an analysis of the index, beginning with 1955, simply noting the number of times, year by year, the indicator changed columns from "X"s to "O"s suggesting rising prices vs. falling prices respectively.

The result of that study: 62% of the time there were only 2 to 4 shifts between supply and demand and 27% of the time there were between 5 and 7 shifts. However, you should know that in 2008 the shifts between supply and demand occurred 13 times!

While this was THE extreme over the 57 years; in 1960 and 2011 there were 10 shifts and in 2010 there were 9 shifts.

No one, in my opinion, can navigate 13 - 10 - 9 or even 5 jumps in and out of the market which is why I embrace relative strength as a much better measure for managing the risk of catastrophic losses. So far in 2013, we've had 5 shifts. Again, in my opinion, 5 is too many to jump.

Yet, When I was first introduced to this indicator, a few decades ago, it WAS viewed as an on off switch. Reversals down were a reason for caution and in some cases increasing the cash balances in portfolios. At least that's the way I interpreted it.

So if the the principal of Point & Figure technical analysis it to point at data and figure the implications, then I feel it is appropriate to believe what the data is telling us. It is for this reason I believe it is worthwhile to look at not only the NYSE but the following populations as well.

1. The Bullish Percent For Optionable Stock Universe: this population includes stocks upon which put and call options are publicly traded.

2. The Bullish Percent For OTC Stock Universe: this population includes stocks traded on an over the counter exchange.

3. The Bullish Percent for the S&P 500 index: this population includes the 500 stocks included in the index.

4. The Bullish Percent For the NASDAQ: this population includes all the stocks included in the index.

Looking at these Bullish Percents individually and collectively give, in my opinion a broader perspective on the "Market".

The Bullish Percent concept is also applied to individual industries as well. Stocks are divided into forty groups from Aerospace/Airlines to Waste Management. Again, it's just another way to look at the "Market". This is known as Sector Analysis.

The point is to review as much or as little real data as necessary to make logical, organized, systematic decisions about the real direction of today's markets.

All I can ever know is what the market is telling me today.

Will it remain the same for the rest of the year? I have no idea.

What I do know from 30 years of experience is when things change, the market will let me know, provided I look and listen to what it's saying.

Do I care about retail sales data - not really; do I care about how many days the Dow inches up - not really. Do I care about the fiscal cliff, sequester, asian markets, sugar subsidy, Pope Francis - not really.

All I care about is if supply or demand is in control of the markets where my money is working. The rest is "news" at best and entertainment at worst.

The very first step - every day... is to answer this simple question:
"Is this a market worthy of my investment capital?"

If you remember only one thing from this entire book, remember this: "Is this a market worthy of my investment capital?" is not a question mutual fund managers ask because their job is to give investors exposure to a fairly specific investment category. They leave it up to YOU to determine THEIR place in YOUR investment strategy.

I saw an interview of Barry Ritholtz, the CEO and director of equity research at online quantitative research firm Fusion IQ, one of the few strategists who saw the 2008 housing implosion and derivative mess far in advance.

He was asked: What is your outlook on the markets and the economy? Here is what he said:

"Let me begin with an answer you will hate: My opinion as to the future state of the economy or where the market might be going will be of no value to your readers. Indeed, as my blog readers will tell you, I doubt anyone's perspectives on these issues are of any value whatsoever."

He then goes on to say:

"given the plethora of conflicting conjectures in the financial firmament, how can any reader determine which author to believe and which to ignore? You can find an opinion to confirm any prior view, which is a typical reason why many investors make erroneous decisions."

And finally he says, and this speaks to the point we were just discussing:

"studies have shown that the most confident, specific and detailed forecasts about the future are: a.) most likely to be believed by readers and TV viewers; and b.) least likely to be correct."

401(k) computer models, using modern portfolio theory, generating the ever-ready pie-chart and asset allocation suggestions are confident, specific and detailed - and wrong. Why the industry still insists on using them is a complete mystery to me.

Barry then states what we've been talking about all along. And I quote

"I would much rather look at the present state of the markets/economy than guess about the future. Most people have no idea what happened yesterday. How on earth can they tell you what is going to happen tomorrow?"

xoxoxo

Positive Trend Analysis

Another way to get a sense of the "Market" is a raw count of industry groups demonstrating a positive trend. As in the Sector Analysis just mentioned, this population consists of forty industry groups.

What we are measuring is the number of stocks in each group which are on a positive trend on their Point & Figure Chart. The individual groups are analyzed to determine if the population is demonstrating rising positive trend or a falling positive trend. The number of groups showing a positive trend are then tallied and posted on a chart similar to a Bullish Percent Chart.

I only mention this type of analysis to let you know it exists. You will not find it for free online. It is a subscription product available to investment professionals. You may hear me mention it from time to time on The 401(k) Owners Manual Podcast.

xoxoxo

Relative Strength Analysis

In the previous discussion of the top five mutual funds found in 401(k) plans, you may be interested to know that the top 10 stocks found in those mutual funds at the time were Comcast; Amazon; Google; Coke; Wells Fargo; Berkshire Hathaway; Oracle; Exxon; Microsoft; and, Apple.

I'm going to introduce a different form of technical analysis which is based on the Point & Figure methodology. It's called "Relative Strength" and we are going to use the top 10 stocks I just mentioned to illustrate the point.

Before we reveal what Relative Strength is all about, think about what you've typically heard from the "experts." Have you ever heard a mutual fund manager or your broker say "we've outperformed the market"?

You may have even heard those words uttered in 2008. "We only lost 40% and the market was down 50% so we outperformed."

We both know you can't spend that kind of outperformance.

Relative Strength is the idea that given a number of investment choices, you can measure the performance of each, setting one in direct competition against another, one by one, through every choice, so that the strongest will rise to the top.

Here's how it works: an investment's relative strength can improve if it rises more than it's peers in a market uptrend, or goes down less in a market downtrend.

This is all well and good; however, it assumes the goal is to be invested at all times and in all markets. If the last 13 years has taught you anything, it's this: being invested at all times and in all markets is not a risk free strategy.

So, let's consider taking a good idea and doing what we can reasonably do to make it better. Consider this: suppose we take the basic concept of pitting each investment choice against one another AND include in the mix another investment alternative, the one Wall Street doesn't want you to ever think about, cash.

Well, not really cash; but something close to a money market return, a 13 Week Treasury Bill.

So here we go.

Taking the top ten stocks we mentioned earlier and adding to the mix a substitute for cash we are ready to do our analysis.

The simplest way to view the competition is to arrange the results in tabular form.

We have eleven rows containing the investment alternatives and columns titled:

RANK	TICKER	NAME	BUYS	Xs
		Rankings as of 12/14/2012		
1	CMCSA	Comcast Corporation	10	9
2	AMZN	Amazon.com Inc.	9	8
3	GOOG	Google Inc.	8	3
4	KO	The Coca-Cola Company	6	4
5	WFC	Wells Fargo & Company	6	4
6	BRK.A	Berkshire Hathaway Inc.	4	7
7	ORCL	Oracle Corporation	3	8
8	XOM	Exxon Mobile Corporation	3	5
9	MSFT	Microsoft Corporation	3	1
10	MNYMKT	13 week T-Bill	1	6
11	AAPL	Apple Inc.	1	0

Rank, Ticker, Name, Buys and Xs.

The column headings: Rank, Ticker, and Name need no explanation. However, we need to focus on the headings: Buys and Xs.

All we're doing here is measuring the number of times one investment has proven a relative strength win vs. one of the other alternative investments. We are looking at two criteria. The first criteria is <u>current</u> relative strength and the second is a somewhat longer term, historical view of the relative strength relationship.

Remember, an investment's relative strength can improve if it rises <u>more than</u> the challenger in a market uptrend, or goes down <u>less than</u> the challenger in a market downtrend.

This is a simple filter. It either is or it is not. The current relative strength totals are presented in the column titled "X"s. The longer term, historical relative strength totals are presented in the column titled "Buys."

As in the case of traditional Point & Figure charts, these "Buys" are <u>not</u> a call to action. It is not a recommendation. It's jargon used by a Point & Figure chartist.

Let's first focus on the results based on the <u>current</u> relative strength rankings. The top three slots have been taken by Comcast; Amazon and Oracle. Why? Because Comcast has captured nine relative strength wins vs. the competition while both Amazon and Oracle have each captured eight wins.

RANK	TICKER	NAME	Xs
		Rankings as of 12/14/2012	
1	CMCSA	Comcast Corporation	9
2	AMZN	Amazon.com Inc.	8
3	ORCL	Oracle Corporation	8
4	BRK.A	Berkshire Hathaway Inc.	7
5	MNYMKT	13 week T-Bill	6
6	XOM	Exxon Mobile Corporation	5
7	KO	The Coca-Cola Company	4
8	WFC	Wells Fargo & Company	4
9	GOOG	Google Inc.	3
10	MSFT	Microsoft Corporation	1
11	AAPL	Apple Inc.	0

Note the 13 week T-Bill has captured a 5th place slot because it's <u>currently</u> outperforming the six alternatives below it. In other words, you would be better off, <u>currently</u> holding money market assets vs. any one of the 6 potential investments below <u>including</u> Google and Apple.

Now let's focus on the results based on the longer term, historical relative strength rankings. Here, the top three slots have been taken by Comcast, Amazon and Google. Note also the 13 week T-Bill has fallen to the 10th place slot because the only alternative below it is Apple.

		Rankings as of 12/14/2012	
RANK	TICKER	NAME	BUYS
1	CMCSA	Comcast Corporation	10
2	AMZN	Amazon.com Inc.	9
3	GOOG	Google Inc.	8
4	KO	The Coca-Cola Company	6
5	WFC	Wells Fargo & Company	6
6	BRK.A	Berkshire Hathaway Inc.	4
7	ORCL	Oracle Corporation	3
8	XOM	Exxon Mobile Corporation	3
9	MSFT	Microsoft Corporation	3
10	MNYMKT	13 week T-Bill	1
11	AAPL	Apple Inc.	1

The takeaway here is... it's certainly possible for an investment to be on a buy signal even though it's currently demonstrating weakness. We continuously measure these data points because it is possible for the short term trend to become the long term trend.

How an investor chooses to make use of current data has to do with his or her investment horizon (how long it will be before they need the money) and tolerance for risk (how large an unrealized loss they can emotionally handle).

From my perspective, particularly when evaluating investment alternatives in a 401(k) plan, this is valuable information. Owning a highly regarded investment with poor relative strength is like owning the best horse in the glue factory.

Remember, equity research analysts, mutual fund rating agencies, credit rating agencies, stock brokers, registered investment advisors, fund managers and the financial media ALL have a vested interest in what they are selling.

Warren Buffett once said: "Many in Wall Street (a community in which quality control is not prized) will sell investors anything they will buy."

My personal observation over the years can only confirm his statement. Let the buyer beware. Make no mistake, there are no disinterested parties when it comes to investment recommendations.

Do I have a vested interest in presenting these ideas? Absolutely. The only difference is, in my opinion, these ideas are transparent. Given the same data points, anyone versed in Point and Figure charting will see the same thing. How they choose and how you choose to use it... is up to you.

The ideas expressed here are to present objective tools to provide a logical organized systematic way to measure supply and demand so you can break down barriers to making better 401(k) investment choices.

Chapter Eight
Final Thoughts

Awareness, Acceptance, Action

If I have achieved my goal I have helped you understand:

1. Some disturbing information about your 401(k),
2. Some disturbing information about the industry and,
3. Some useful solutions to overcome the obstacles to your retirement readiness.

I'll leave you with this story...

It wasn't that long ago I saw a quote by Warren Buffett which has stuck with me to this day: In his Chairman's letter from the year 2000 he said " a pin lies in wait for every bubble. And when the two eventually meet, a new wave of investors learn some very old lessons: First, many in Wall Street - a community in which quality control is not prized - will sell investors anything they will buy. Second, speculation is most dangerous when it looks easiest."

And so is history about to repeat itself? I saw an article on CNN's Money channel. The title "Get nearly free 401(k) advise at work" the subtitle was "It's the best-kept secret in 401(k)s: free or low cost professional advice"

The author actually states "for many workers professional advice starts and stops with Target Date Funds..." How this author can be so misinformed as to actually believe this product constitutes professional advice is just beyond my comprehension. It's a product. A product with a recurring fee. A product which uses a flawed investment strategy and, insult to injury, executes the strategy poorly.

The author goes on to suggest: and I quote

"For a cost of 0.2% to 0.7% of assets a year (on top of investment fees), you'll get a customized mix of your plan's mutual funds geared to your goals and risk tolerance, either run by the plan's investment provider or an outside adviser, such as Financial Engines, Guided Choice, or Merrill Lynch."

Allow me to repeat myself, what you are getting here hardly rises to the level of professional advice because you are getting a product, again with a recurring fee, which is delivering a flawed investment strategy based on modern portfolio theory. If the theory worked, you would not have lost 40 to 60% of your 401(k) in 2008. Period. At the very time the theory was supposed to work, it failed... gloriously.

What shakes me is this kind of article gains traction and settles into the public psyche. Monday, my twitter fed was jammed with retweets of this article.

This kind of reporting is nothing new and I guess I should be immune to it by now. But it has an impact.

I remember working on a charity board and was talking with a fellow board member, a medical doctor, about the charity's investments in mutual funds. When I suggested a registered investment advisor who's investment philosophy is not unlike my own, this Doctor was shocked. You mean they will be buying and selling stocks? Isn't that market timing? She said.

I very gently asked her what she thought was happening inside the mutual fund. She said I don't know but they believe in buy and hold. She was dumbfounded when I showed her how frequently they were trading stocks inside the fund, the fees they were charging and the overall poor performance relative to the benchmark index as well as other managers.

Needless to say we had several more conversations; but, I don't think she ever really shook the marketing messages which had been imprinted on her brain.

The takeaway for you is, just take a moment to look for the incentives and judge for yourself.

You now have tools to easily look at retirement in a whole new way.

Do you have an idea of what your retirement might look like? Have you spent time imagining all the wonderful things you will do? Have you imagined where you would like to live? Have you imagined who will be with you?

Does it make sense that there is someone who will pay you to do what you absolutely love; and, that that person is you? Is it possible to look at saving for retirement as a gift you are giving yourself?

Can you spend a little time calmly reviewing charts of your portfolio investments on a regular basis? Can you free yourself from the drama of financial media; or, at least view it as entertainment?

Try the methodology for a time and see if it works for you because that is the ultimate test. Do you feel more confident in holding your investments despite whatever drama is being touted in the mass media? If you are not prepared to do this all alone, feel free to contact me. I will reply to you personally.

You deserve to have stability and security.

Today is a good day to start. Now is even better.